A Call from Egypt

A Jewish Woman's Search for Her Muslim Family

A Memoir

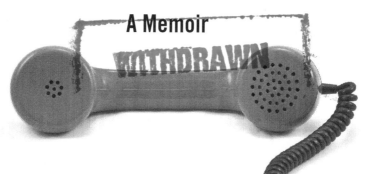

Joan Kadri Zald

ISBN: 1484139607
ISBN 13: 9781484139608
Library of Congress Control Number: 2013909792
CreateSpace Independent Publishing Platform
North Charleston, South Carolina

In loving memory of my husband, Mayer,

and for our children

Ann, David, and Harold.

The events in this story primarily occurred during a five-year period, from 1975 to 1980. As with most stories involving families, roots established much earlier in time influenced the course of later events.

Recently, my increased awareness of the passage of time and the continuing interest and encouragement of family and friends motivated me, after so many years, to finally tell this story.

In order to write an accurate account, I revisited materials (letters, legal documents, journals, and a tape recording) that I had saved but had not looked at for decades. They transported me back in time, and I was flooded with memories, some of them quite vivid, as if it had all occurred yesterday. The process of looking back not only revived memories but also enabled me to see many things in a new and different light and, for the first time, to fit together some of the missing pieces.

Chapters

Rosenblum Family

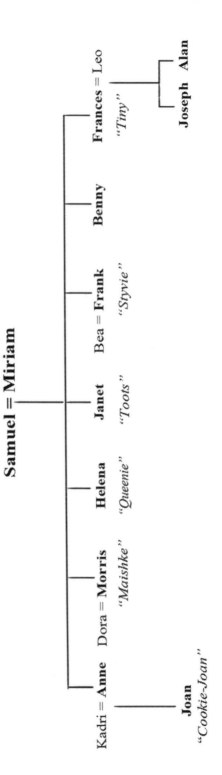

The Phone Call

It all started with a phone call. My husband, Mayer, and I were living in Nashville at the time. I was home alone with our youngest child, Harold, who, as I start to write this, is thirty-six years old and was then an infant. The caller identified himself by saying, "My name is Mr. Courchaine and I am calling from the Canadian embassy in Washington, DC, on behalf of your stepmother." I remember being puzzled and responding that I was sorry there was some mistake. He had called the wrong person, as I had no stepmother. "Your stepmother in Egypt," he added. *Oh, Egypt.* I asked him to tell me more.

It became clear that he had reached the right person. The gist of what he related in our conversation was that my father, known in the United States as Arthur Kadri and in Egypt as Abdullah Kadri Khalil El Lamie, had recently died in Cairo. (As I had lost contact with him years before, I thought my father had already been dead for at least twelve years prior to this phone call.) His widow, Olwen (I hadn't known he had a second wife), was almost destitute due to my father's brothers blocking her from inheriting any of his estate. She knew of my existence and was hoping I could be located and help her with her lawsuit against them. A Canadian citizen, she had gone to the Canadian embassy in Cairo requesting their help in finding me. My University of Michigan Phi Beta Kappa key had been found among my father's possessions (I had wondered what had happened to it and didn't know that my father had taken it) and was used in the search. The Canadian embassy in DC had contacted the University of Michigan Alumni Association, and they had provided my address and phone number. At the end of the phone conversation, I told Mr. Courchaine that I was open to receiving a letter from Olwen and learning more about her situation and the kind of help she wanted from me. It was a lot of information to absorb at one time.

———•••••———

The last time I had seen my father (who everyone called Kadri as if it was his first name) was at my wedding seventeen years earlier, in 1958. He had been going back and forth to Egypt quite a bit during my undergraduate and graduate years. The reasons for the trips were never clear to me other than he claimed he had to attend to business matters. He returned to New York City a few days before my wedding and flew back to Egypt the day after, for what eventually did become clear, was his final breakup with my mother, Anne. I don't know what had transpired between them before he left, and neither of them had prepared me for his leave-taking.

I did not find out about his departure until weeks after I had returned to my home in Ann Arbor. I remember feeling extremely hurt that he had not told me he was leaving permanently and that he had not said good-bye. My mother, typically, never discussed with me what had gone on between them and I knew enough not to ask.

My mother died two years after the wedding. While I was cleaning out her apartment, I found a letter from Kadri that he had written to her five months after his departure. It was an angry, accusatory, final good-bye letter. In it he said, "I never imagined things would turn out the way they had but it was not my choice. You have done a terrible thing. You never respected what I stand for. I have every right to be dreadfully angry with you. You never tried to make it up to me by helping daughter (me) understand my views. You on purpose broke up our home. You can now reap what you plant." He added a postscript, "I would love to have a few pictures of Joan's wedding."

I thought his statement about Anne not helping me understand his views to be related, at least in small part, to the request he made to her shortly after his return from Egypt. He wanted Mayer and me to get married at the Egyptian consulate in New York City. His stated reason was that this was a way to ensure that I could inherit his land in Egypt after his death. I had some awareness at the time that his family owned rich agricultural land along the Nile. My mother didn't give this request much credence, and he never raised the idea with me. She probably saw it as being similar to other requests he used to make, among them wanting me to marry a particular nephew of his in Egypt. When she did finally tell me of his wish that I get married at the consulate, I thought the idea ludicrous and didn't appreciate its importance to him until many years later.

My mother had been my wedding planner. I was twenty-two years old at the time and was away in graduate school in Ann Arbor. She made arrangements for a traditional Jewish wedding ceremony at a large, prominent synagogue in Manhattan with a sit-down meal, a dance band, and all the other trimmings. Mayer and I, both of us Jewish but non-observant, which was also true of my mother, would have preferred a secular wedding ceremony rather than one performed by a conservative rabbi. We also would have preferred a less elaborate wedding, and I wondered if Anne had gone into debt to pay for it all. But I didn't protest too much as she seemed to want it so badly. It was as if she was making up for the wedding she never had. I knew my parents had gotten married in a civil ceremony in a New York City courthouse. I don't think there had been any family or friends in attendance. I also thought my Jewish wedding was a gift to her parents. My father, a Muslim, was the odd man out.

My mother's parents, Miriam and Samuel Rosenblum, were Orthodox Jews, who as a young couple emigrated from Poland to the United States in order to escape the pogroms of the time. My mother and her younger brother, Morris, were both born in Poland, and she was two or three years old when they arrived in this country in the early 1900s. The family settled in New York City where Samuel worked as a tailor in the garment industry. In Poland, he had dreamed of becoming either a tailor or a carpenter.

They had a total of seven children over the course of fourteen years. The five youngest were born in quick succession after their arrival in the United States. The family lived for decades in cramped tenement apartments in Manhattan's Lower East Side. Relatives and "landsmen" (fellow Jews from the same district or town) often stayed with them after arriving in the United States, making for even more crowded conditions. Most of those relatives eventually moved on to Chicago. All the family members who remained in Poland were, decades later, annihilated in the Holocaust.

My grandparents spoke Yiddish and never mastered English. They had received little formal education in Poland but could read and write Yiddish, and my grandfather had acquired some proficiency in Hebrew from his early religious training. Yiddish was my mother's first language, and she learned English once she started attending elementary school. She became the family's ambassador; she translated for her parents, taught her younger siblings English, and helped them navigate beyond their Jewish immigrant neighborhood.

Similar to many Jewish immigrants of their time, the family was upwardly mobile and education was highly valued. Despite their poverty, my mother and four of her siblings were able to attend college, as the New York City college system at that time charged no tuition. On the whole, they were a very accomplished bunch, and three of them were especially creative. My uncle Morris, after many years of teaching foreign languages in Brooklyn high schools, obtained a PhD in classics and eventually taught at Columbia University. He was the author and co-author of numerous books. My mother, Anne, an elementary school teacher in the New York City public school system, obtained a master's degree in art history and became an accomplished amateur painter, studying at the Art Students League in New York City and spending some summers taking art classes in San Miguel Allende in Mexico. My aunt Janet, who initially worked as a secretary at a furniture company and had a wonderful sense of design, started her own furniture company, specializing in modern, Scandinavian-style office furniture. We still have furniture in our home that she made for us decades ago.

<hr />

As the family prospered, Samuel and Miriam bought a two-story semidetached house in the Allerton Avenue neighborhood in the Bronx, which became the center of family activity. My mother and I lived with my grandparents in that house the first two years of my life while my father was in Egypt. My very earliest memory takes place in that house. It is of being coaxed by my grandmother, as I must have been somewhat wary, to go into the sun parlor to meet my father for the first time. She held my hand and drew me along saying, "Come, Cookala, don't be afraid, come meet your father."

Upon Kadri's return, my parents moved to a one-bedroom apartment in a six-story apartment building that was directly across the street from my grandparents' house. I slept in the living room, and the apartment felt cramped in comparison to my grandparents' house. I recall having to keep all my playthings in one cardboard box, which was put away in a hall closet every night and whenever guests were expected. My mother remained in that apartment for the rest of her life. Throughout my childhood, I spent a good deal of my time with my grandparents and aunts and uncles who were in and out of the family home.

Hard-working Italian and Eastern European Jewish immigrants and their families primarily populated the Allerton Avenue neighborhood. The streets were lined with two-story semidetached houses similar to the one my grandparents owned, along with some single-family dwellings and apartment buildings, usually no more than six stories high. Allerton Avenue, a long commercial thoroughfare that included an elevated subway station, was bordered on the west by Bronx Park and on the east by heavily trafficked Boston Post Road. The trains that stopped at the station were the neighborhood's primary public transportation link to Manhattan and the other boroughs.

There were two institutions of note at the Bronx Park end of the avenue. One was the Beth Abraham Home for Incurables (an awful name!) and the other was "the Coops." The Home for Incurables was familiar to me because the synagogue in Beth Abraham was available to the neighboring Jewish community. It was where my grandparents attended High Holiday services, along with the patients from the Home for Incurables who were able to attend. It was also a place where my grandmother did volunteer work.

The Coops was a residential housing complex that took up two square city blocks and had been built in the 1920s by the United Workers Cooperative Colony. It was a co-op community composed of radicals and progressives and was a magnet for communists, socialists, anarchists, and their sympathizers. It also served as a haven for black and bi-racial families who were unable to gain access to housing in other middle-class neighborhoods. Over time, the complex was taken over by private owners, and the political climate of the complex changed as new residents moved in. My mother had once thought of enrolling me in the nursery school in the Coops. Upon visiting and seeing the portraits of Lenin and Stalin adorning the walls and the hammers and sickles on all the doors, she quickly changed her mind. A number of my schoolmates lived in the Coops, and their families experienced considerable stress during the McCarthy witch hunts. There were frequent rumors that residents of the Coops were being investigated for un-American activities, and some residents, including parents of some of my friends, did lose their jobs due to the rampant unsubstantiated accusations and insinuations of the era.

Allerton Avenue had one movie theater, one bank, pharmacies, a beauty parlor, a barbershop, a five-and-dime store, and numerous ethnic butcher shops, bakeries, grocery stores, and delicatessens. When I was in elementary school, my best friend, Arlene, and I would spend our Saturday afternoons at the neighborhood theater. The theater's Saturday matinees catered to children and offered cartoons and adventure serials as well as a feature film. After school on nice days, we would stroll up and down the street eating sour pickles selected from wooden barrels from one of the Jewish delicatessens or licking ices bought at an Italian bakery. During the day, the noise of the streets—neighbors sitting on their stoops talking to one another, voices of children playing stickball, "potsy," or jumping rope, mothers calling out their windows for their children to come home, delivery trucks rumbling by, car horns honking—dominated, but at night the roar of traffic on Boston Post Road and the clanging of the trains entering and leaving the station came to the fore and lulled me to sleep.

I was an only child and for twelve years my grandparents' sole grandchild. Miriam and Samuel gave me the attention they had not been able to sufficiently bestow on their own children, probably due to the number of children they had in quick succession and their early years of poverty and struggles to adapt to a new country. Despite the fact that my spoken Yiddish was poor, I was always able to communicate with them. I understood their Yiddish and they in turn seemed to have no trouble comprehending my patois of English and Yiddish.

I was close to both grandparents but was particularly close to my grandmother. She gave me her unconditional love, was sensitive to my feelings, and had the ability to soothe and comfort me. It was a very special relationship and served as the emotional bedrock of my early life. Miriam was a poorly educated woman who didn't seem to have much curiosity about the world at large, although she always cared about the welfare of others. Her days were primarily taken up with household tasks—grocery shopping, cooking, baking, and cleaning. She went grocery shopping almost daily on Allerton Avenue in order to buy fresh produce, meat, or poultry. Everything she cooked and baked was made from scratch. In her free time she read the daily Yiddish language newspaper, *The Forward.* She particularly liked the serialized stories and the "Bintel Brief," an advice column that was initially started to help East European Jewish immigrants adapt to their new country. To me, her life seemed insular and constricted; most of her time was spent at home and she never ventured by herself outside the neighborhood.

My mother was very different from my grandmother. Although Anne was short in stature (she was slightly under five feet) and had suffered from rickets due to malnutrition in childhood, she had a commanding presence. She also had suffered from an episode of Bell's palsy (a paralysis of the facial nerve), which left her with some residual paralysis on the right side of her face. Based on family photographs, I think this must have occurred when she was in her late thirties or early forties because after that age she avoided having her picture taken, and when it couldn't be avoided, she turned the left side of her face to the camera.

Anne lacked my grandmother's nurturing abilities, but had many qualities that I came to appreciate as I grew older. In contrast to Miriam, she was creative, intellectually stimulating, very well read, and well informed about social and political issues. She was also open to new experiences and adventures, had traveled widely, and I was told that she was considered a bohemian in her younger days. Anne was very concerned about social and economic inequalities and would occasionally take me along to lectures dealing with such issues, lectures that were way beyond my level of comprehension at the time. She was also committed to exposing me to the arts via lessons and by taking me to exhibits, concerts, and the theater—things she had been denied in her own childhood. Although Anne lacked a maternal softness, I knew that she loved me and that she was totally committed to my welfare.

Anne also had a good sense of humor and when she was relaxed, which unfortunately wasn't often enough, could be great fun. I recall times when we were both overcome by the humor of a situation and would collapse into laughing fits. I remember, with some amusement, one such occasion on a subway ride when we couldn't contain our laughter and our fellow passengers kept looking askance at us.

I saw my mother as being a woman of great strength and fortitude who had the courage of her convictions. For instance, due to the proximity of the Coops, it was not unusual during the McCarthy era for FBI agents, in search of communists and communist sympathizers, to appear unexpectedly at our door wanting information from Anne about the politics of our neighbors. I think they selected my mother because she was a teacher in the local school and knew so many of the families. Those were intimidating times, but she never appeared threatened by these visits (although she may have been), and she consistently refused to discuss the political beliefs of neighbors with the federal agents. However, there were occasions when others were fearful of speaking out, when she openly and courageously defended those whom she believed were being falsely accused. Although I never thought about it when I was young, it certainly must have taken courage on her part to marry a non-Jew, since it went against the dictates of her Jewish family and community.

I heard many stories told in my grandparents' social circle about Orthodox Jewish families who disowned their children when they married outside the faith, as my mother had done. They mourned them as dead and had no contact with them or the children from those unions. I doubted my grandparents ever considered doing such a thing. I can't conceive of them being willing to renounce their daughter or granddaughter; we were far too important to them. Although my grandparents' relationship with my father was distant, as best as I can recall, they treated him cordially on the rare occasions when he attended family dinners at their house. Since my grandparents' English was minimal and my father spoke no Yiddish, conversations between them tended to be limited.

I never felt the fact that I was a daughter of a Muslim affected my grandparents' feelings for me. Occasionally, in a fit of annoyance or anger, usually because I hadn't been to visit her for a few days, Miriam would accuse me of acting like a "goy" (Yiddish for gentile or non-Jew), a pejorative term for her. I never took it to heart and knew a hug or kiss from me would quickly dispel her fit of pique.

One of my poignant memories of my grandmother dates back to one Christmas season. The Italian families in the neighborhood all had Christmas trees displayed in their windows during the holidays. Oh, how I loved the trees and yearned for one. My mother made it clear in no uncertain terms, year after year, that we would not have a Christmas tree. One year I made a greater fuss than usual and Miriam, aware of my disappointment, went to the neighborhood five-and-dime store and bought me a gift of a small, ten- to fifteen-inch plastic Christmas tree. Even though I was a child at the time, I appreciated that love had trumped religious orthodoxy.

To this day, I am still affected by the smells I associate with Miriam. Many years after her death, I had an experience that brought this home to me. I was in a meeting with a professional colleague when I suddenly felt an overwhelming rush of affection for her. Although I liked and respected the woman, the intensity and suddenness of my feelings puzzled me. It took me a while to realize that the smell of a tar-based salve that emanated from her had aroused my emotions. My grandmother suffered from psoriasis and daily used a similar-smelling salve. Since childhood I have connected that smell with her and always found it pleasurable and comforting.

Although I received no formal religious education, I absorbed a great deal from my grandparents as both an observer and participant in their religious practices. Miriam followed strict kosher dietary laws and they punctiliously observed the Sabbath. While I still lived at home before I went off to college, I would attend High Holiday services at my grandparents' synagogue. I did this to oblige my grandmother, who requested that I sit with her during the daylong services. The men and women sat separately, the services were lengthy and tired her, and she seemed to derive energy and pleasure from my company. During Passover, I always participated in the seders conducted by my grandfather.

I also picked up, almost by osmosis, the concept of tikkun olam from the family. It is a Hebrew phrase meaning "repairing the world," and one contemporary interpretation is that of making the world a better place through social action, charitable giving, and acts of kindness. I am sure this value system partially contributed to my eventual choice of social work as a career. My mother and two of her brothers, Morris and Benny, were political activists, involved in supporting workers' rights as well as what today would be considered social justice issues. Samuel had set an example for his children by his active participation in the ILGWU (International Ladies' Garment Workers' Union), a union started in the early part of the twentieth century and known for its efforts in protecting the rights of workers.

It was Miriam, however, whose example left an indelible impression on me. For years, one day out of every week, she walked many city blocks (no small feat for an elderly woman with bunions) to the Beth Abraham Home for Incurables on Bronx River Parkway. She spent the entire day as a volunteer helping to feed patients and talking, reading, and socializing with those who spoke Yiddish. A considerable number of the patients had deformities that caused most people (myself included) to turn away. Miriam seemed able to look beyond their disfigurements and see their humanity. My friend Arlene shared with me years ago that Miriam's volunteer work had left a powerful impression on her, as it had on me, and helped steer her toward her own service activities in adulthood.

———

Only four of Miriam and Samuel's seven children married and only two had children. My uncle Benny had given nicknames to family members, with the exception of his two oldest siblings, my mother Anne and my uncle Morris (whom the family often called by his Yiddish name, Maishke). Most of the nicknames caught on and were used by everyone in the family. Janet was called "Toots" or "Tootsie" because she was tough, Frank was "Styvie" because he had gone to Stuyvesant High School, Frances was "Tiny" as she was the youngest, although she ended up being the tallest. Benny also created nicknames—"Shorty" and "Shortboy-small"—for Frances's two sons, Joseph and Alan, but aside from Benny, no one else in the family called them by those names. In contrast, everyone used the names Benny had bestowed on me—"Cookie" or sometimes "Cookie-Joan." My grandparents came up with a Yiddish-sounding and affectionate version and often called me "Cookala." Those nicknames stayed with me well into my college years. In fact, my friend Arlene recalls that I emphatically requested that she drop the "Cookie" part of "Cookie-Joan" when we were in college.

My family was different from most regarding the norms concerning how children should address adult family members. With the exception of my grandparents, I called adults in the family by their first names (no aunt or uncle prefixes), and it was never viewed as being disrespectful. It therefore seemed natural for me to sometimes call my aunts and uncles by the nicknames Benny had given them. My two younger cousins followed my example.

Despite their commitment to tikkun olam, some family members did not treat one another with kindness. My aunt Lena (or Helena) was the loose cannon in the family. Benny called her "Queenie" because of her bossiness and critical nature. In later years, he also referred to her, sometimes even to her face, as "The Psycho" because of her increasing tendency to provoke fights with family members and her frequent negative and deprecating criticism of others. My mother usually called her "Q" and I always called her Queenie. Even my young children would call her Queenie—one just couldn't think of her as anything else, and her given name fell into disuse. The animosity between my father and Queenie was great, and at one point in time he insisted she not be allowed to enter our apartment. My mother honored his wishes, so I assume Queenie must have been more offensive than usual.

Queenie was very loyal and attached to my mother and frequently criticized me for not being a good enough daughter. Her criticisms were usually off the wall. One that I often heard in my childhood was that I had caused my mother to have a painful and difficult childbirth leading to a Cesarean section. Queenie said it as if I had willfully done so. I knew enough not to take that one seriously, but sometimes her criticisms hurt even when they were irrational. For instance, she accused me of having caused my mother's mouth cancer by not writing to her often enough; she was of course ignoring the fact that my mother had been a pack-a-day smoker all her adult life. Queenie appeared to have no awareness of other people's feelings or how her behavior affected and alienated others. In writing this today, I realize that she was not only an angry and bitter woman but a deeply unhappy one as well.

My aunts and uncles were important people in my life. In particular, Frances, Janet, Frank, and Benny, although not prone to emotional demonstrativeness, were positive and caring. They played with me when I was young and often took me with them on outings when I was older. Frank was an avid Yankees fan, and we often went to ball games at Yankee Stadium or watched the games on TV together. Benny, whose avocation was locating out-of-print books people commissioned him to find, would sometimes take me along as he scoured small independent bookstores for the books he sought. Janet invited me to go with her to concerts of baroque music and to furniture shows, and one year when I was in high school, she hired me to be her "assistant" in her showroom. Frances was less available to me during my teenage years, as she was then married, the mother of two young sons, and lived in Queens. I found her, of all my mother's siblings, to be a very good listener and the most empathic.

My grandfather also enjoyed taking me with him on outings. He was a man of intelligence and curiosity who liked to explore the synagogues and the different forms of Jewish worship in the city. He also was a big fan of Charlie Chaplin movies, and we would go to see them together whenever they were showing in Manhattan.

In addition to Queenie, Morris was the other adult in the Rosenblum family with whom I had a difficult relationship, although I was very fond of his wife, Dora. He frequently found ways to criticize or belittle me. I recall one time at a family gathering at our apartment when he saw a certificate on my bulletin board for a high school geometry award that I had won. Upon seeing it, he proclaimed to the gathering that any idiot who could use a compass and a ruler could get such an award. This was not atypical of his behavior toward me. I had felt proud of the award and found his remarks painful and insulting. He often spoke in glowing terms of the accomplishments and "smarts" of Miriam, his good friend Leo's daughter, who was approximately my age. There always was the implication that I could never measure up to her.

Years later at his funeral, a few of Morris's former graduate students were among the speakers and praised him for being a supportive and caring teacher and mentor. My cousin Alan was at the funeral with me, and after the service we shared our astonishment that Morris had been so described. Neither of us recognized the man they had portrayed. I became aware for the first time that although he hadn't been as nasty to my cousins Joseph and Alan as he had been to me, he hadn't been kind to them either.

When I was older, I wondered why he held such ill will toward me and I came to the conclusion that it was rooted in earlier family relationships. I thought he resented me because my grandparents had doted on me and had given me so much more love and attention than he had received. I also thought another source of resentment, which ended being directed at me, was the fact that that my mother (clearly more of a favorite with Miriam and Samuel than he) had a child whereas he and his wife were unable to have children.

In the last few years of his life when he was ailing, Morris requested that I visit him whenever I was in New York. The better part of my nature usually prevailed and I would go to see him. It was clear to me that although his cognitive functioning was fine, he had absolutely no awareness of how shabbily he had treated me when I was young.

It was not until I went away to college and observed how the families of my college friends communicated that I became aware of how dysfunctional the communication patterns in the Rosenblum family were. I never observed my grandparents speaking to one another; they communicated via their children or, as I grew older, through me. They lived in the same house, slept in the same room (albeit in twin beds), and Miriam always took special care cooking for Samuel as he had become diabetic. Yet they never spoke to one another. I was told their marriage had not been arranged by a matchmaker, as was traditional in their Polish shtetl, and that theirs had been a love match. Something had clearly gone amiss at some point; I never knew what, and I don't know if their children knew either.

The pattern of not speaking was replicated in two other relationships. My uncle Morris and my grandfather avoided talking to one another. I don't know how far back that went, but I would guess well before I was born. I was once told that Samuel had been a very authoritarian father who had been tyrannical and abusive to Morris, his eldest son. I think that either my mother or one of her siblings told me this, so I don't doubt its veracity. It was, however, a description of a man very different from the doting grandfather I knew. Morris was also not on speaking terms with his younger brother Benny.

I learned from an early age not to ask questions as to why family members behaved the way they did or why they had certain physical problems. Why did some family members not talk to one another? Why did my grandmother have a damaged and blind eye? Why did Queenie walk with a decided limp? Did Benny have a medical problem that caused his facial and body tics? Such questions were frowned upon and went unanswered. Much was left unspoken, and as a result, there seemed to me to be a lot of family secrets. As a child, I sometimes found it difficult to figure out what was acceptable to ask and what wasn't. Despite the apparent animosity in some of the relationships, family members, no longer religiously observant, all showed up on Friday nights for Sabbath candle lighting and dinner, traveling by subway from Brooklyn or Manhattan to the Bronx.

———•◦•◦•———

Anne had always played a central role in her family, seeming to get along well with everyone. Her death in March 1960 was devastating not only to me but to the entire family. She was in her early sixties when she succumbed to cancer. She had been diagnosed with mouth cancer and had undergone surgery less than a year prior to her death. I was twenty-four years old at the time and working in my first job as a social worker in a psychiatric hospital in Michigan. Frances called me to tell me to come home as my mother had suddenly taken a turn for the worse and had been moved to my grandparents' house. Queenie was living with my grandparents at the time and was helping with Anne's care. A few days after my arrival, following a game of Scrabble, a favorite nighttime ritual of ours, my mother said she was tired and went to lie down. I heard a sound that made me think she was vomiting and ran to her room. Blood was gushing from her mouth; I held her as she spewed blood all over both of us and hemorrhaged to death in my arms. Shortly after her death, Sarah, a family friend, said to me, "She waited to die until you came home."

Following the departure of the paramedics who had been called by Queenie while Anne was still hemorrhaging, my grandfather and Queenie started discussing which funeral home to call. Samuel wanted one he knew from his earlier association with Jewish immigrant burial societies. Queenie wanted one that was more modern and assimilated. As I watched, still in a state of shock over my mother's death, Queenie escalated the disagreement into a raging argument, which she eventually ended up winning. My mother probably would have wanted the funeral home Queenie selected, but I recall feeling so pained for my grandfather who had just lost Anne, one of his two favorite children (Frances was the other one), and had to endure Queenie's insensitive, merciless way of handling their decision making.

My mother's casket was left open for viewing at the funeral home prior to the service. I remember entering the viewing room with some trepidation and my grandmother immediately coming over to me to lead me to the casket. Much as she had done when I was an apprehensive two-year-old, she took my hand and said, "Don't be frightened, Cookala, come see your mother."

Immediately after the funeral and while my grandparents were still sitting shivah (a Jewish mourning tradition lasting seven days), my aunts and uncles strongly advised me to postpone writing to Kadri in order to delay informing him of Anne's death. They expressed the opinion that Anne would have wanted me to be her sole heir and would not have wanted my father to benefit financially from her death. They thought she probably had not bothered to leave a will since the bulk of her estate was her teacher's pension and I was listed as the beneficiary. Since my parents were still legally married at the time of her death and there was no will, they suggested I hire a lawyer to help ensure that I inherited everything. Morris recommended a lawyer friend to handle the case for me. They clearly had been preparing themselves, far more than I had, for Anne's death and had been thinking about this issue.

Aside from her pension and some of her belongings, which held sentimental value to me and other family members and friends,

Anne's assets included an old car, furnishings from her three-room apartment, some stocks, a small savings account, and her artwork. The financial value of each of those things was not great and combined were probably equal to the lawyer's fees that I eventually had to pay. The family may have realized this but were committed to preventing Kadri from getting anything. Honoring what they believed to be Anne's wishes was certainly important to them. But I also think the resentment some of them harbored toward Kadri played a role.

I had been unaware of the financial arrangements my parents had while I was growing up. I later came to realize that Anne bore the major financial responsibility for the household and I doubt if Kadri, when he was not living at home, contributed anything. I don't think he helped pay for my college expenses as Anne often had to borrow money from family members to cover them. This may have contributed to their feelings that although my father had a legal right to Anne's estate, he had no moral right.

Some of them were also angry because they believed Kadri had abandoned Anne. Although my allegiance and sympathies were with my mother, I had reservations about their views regarding abandonment. By that time in my life, I was aware that both my parents contributed to their marital problems and thought that Anne had played some role in Kadri's leave taking; he obviously held her totally responsible in his farewell letter.

The family knew I had started corresponding with my father following his return to Egypt. I didn't have his address until he wrote to me five months after my wedding. That letter was brief and I later realized had the same date as the letter he had sent to my mother in which he held her responsible for breaking up their home. I saved both letters and still find poignant the one he wrote to me.

My Dear Joan,

I don't think I shall ever stop loving you.
I can write no more.
I do hope this note finds you and Mayer well and enjoying life. If you have time, do write. I would love to hear what you are both doing and all about you.
I shall never forget your wedding. You were wonderful.

Love,
Kadri

I would love to have some of the wedding pictures.

In my letters to him I kept him informed about what we were doing: my second-year social work internship at a children's psychiatric facility, our new apartment, the university positions Mayer would be applying for after he completed his dissertation, etc. In his letters to me, he primarily responded to what I had written; there was no mention of why he had left nor did he share any information about himself or his life in Cairo. I don't think he ever did receive any of those wedding photos he requested. I regret I was unable to make a special effort to send him some as he continued to make the request in subsequent letters. My mother was the person who had dealt with the photographer and I didn't have the heart to ask her to order photos for him.

———

After the period of sitting shivah, I agreed to follow the advice of my aunts and uncles and postpone writing to Kadri. I also consented to hire Sam Panzer, the lawyer recommended by my uncle. I wanted to respect what the family presented to me as my mother's wishes and what I was sure were their wishes as well. I was also temporarily immobilized by shock and grief and felt incapable of making decisions or dealing with any legal issues. I left it all in the lawyer's hands, and that eventually backfired on me.

Mr. Panzer notified Kadri of Anne's death in a terse legal letter. He immediately got down to business, listed her assets, and asked him to sign a form turning the role of administrator over to me, as well as relinquishing all rights to the estate. He made no mention of Anne's pension but did write that the stocks found in Anne's safe deposit box had been bought for Miriam and Samuel. I assume Queenie had told him that. Kadri was furious and felt that an attempt was being made to disinherit him, and in an angry letter to the lawyer, reminded him that he was the legal heir. In his letter to me he primarily chastised me, saying that I should have been the one who notified him of Anne's death. I felt badly that I hadn't and recognized that he was right.

In his next letter to Mr. Panzer, Kadri indicated awareness of the existence of Anne's pension and accused him and the family of hiding it from him; he also questioned what else was being concealed. Even after he was made aware that I was the legal beneficiary of the pension and that the remaining estate after payment of all liabilities was very small, he continued to vent his rage. A memory, which I held over the years, was that he kept sending me angry letters. In reality, he had never directly expressed anger toward me. I think I remembered it that way because, at the time, I thought he was indirectly attacking me via his continuing ire at the lawyer.

In his letters to me, Kadri frequently made demands that I could not meet, such as wanting me to send him Anne's handwritten directives regarding the disbursement of all her possessions. In one letter he wrote, "Joan, when I receive from you and not your lawyer the complete detailed list of assets and copies of your mother's wishes in her own handwriting, then I will decide <u>what</u> and <u>how</u> I wish to make a waiver. I want to know everything, including the three-room apartment furniture, etc. etc." She had never written such directives. Letters went back and forth dealing with these issues, including his concerns that the Rosenblums would get what he thought was his due.

Kadri, for months on end, refused to sign papers relinquishing his right as administrator as well as claims to the estate. At one point, Mr. Panzer suggested I go to court to testify that Kadri had abandoned Anne and therefore wasn't entitled to anything. I refused to do that, as I doubted that this was an accurate description of what had gone on between them. My lawyer kept prodding me to ask Kadri to sign the papers, which I did many times, uncomfortable as it was to do. Finally, after innumerable requests from me, and a considerable passage of time, he did sign. At no time in these communications did Kadri express sorrow to me about Anne's death. We stopped writing to one another after the legal issues were settled. I think we were both licking our wounds, and I assumed that at some point in the future we would reconnect when emotions cooled.

In looking back, I realize that the situation around Anne's estate had been handled badly. My biggest regret is that I went along with what my aunts and uncles wanted; I abdicated my role in deciding when Kadri would be contacted, who would do the contacting, and how things would be presented to him. I believe that the outcome would have been very different if I had notified Kadri of Anne's death and initiated the discussion about her wishes. I remember being surprised when Mr. Panzer sent me a copy of the letter, which he had already mailed, informing Kadri of Anne's death. He had not checked with me first about who would do the notifying. On the other hand, I had never mentioned to him my desire to be consulted on the matter.

The omission of Anne's pension in the list of assets in Mr. Panzer's initial letter was a mistake. My father knew about the pension and expected that he would be the beneficiary, and perhaps he had been at one time. As a result, he assumed Anne's family was orchestrating nefarious transactions and that other assets were being hidden from him. In retrospect, although I'm sure he would have appreciated receiving the money, I don't think Kadri, once he was informed that I was the beneficiary, begrudged me the pension or the remaining assets. It was the way it had been presented to him that contributed to his anger.

At the time I was puzzled about why he remained so intensely angry, why he kept fighting for a very small amount of money since he was by no means destitute, or why he kept requesting over and over again that I hunt for, and then send him, an itemized list of things Anne had bequeathed to others. After most recently reviewing all the old letters from that time, I now think that Kadri was searching for something from Anne—he wanted to be on her "list." He wanted her to leave him something (anything) that indicated that he was not insignificant, that she still cared for him, respected him, and valued him. But it was not to be found. Not only was he denied that by Anne but by everyone else involved (myself included). I think this caused him much pain and a sense of personal or narcissistic injury. This may have been similar to what he experienced at times in the past and what prompted his very angry letter when they parted. The adage "Hell hath no fury like a woman scorned," with a change of gender, might easily have applied to him.

I finally made the move to reconnect with my father three years later, in 1963, when my daughter Ann (named after my mother) was born. We were then living in Chicago where Mayer was on the faculty of the University of Chicago and I was working as a caseworker at a family service agency. I was ready for a rapprochement, and Ann's birth seemed to offer an ideal opportunity. My father was also the only surviving grandparent my new daughter had. Unfortunately, I had waited too long. The letter, which I sent to Kadri's Cherif Pasha Street address in Cairo, was returned with an "Address Unknown" stamp on the envelope. I thought one explanation, particularly since I hadn't heard from him for so long, was that he had died and his family chose not to let me know. Given his, and I assumed his family's, preoccupation with land inheritance rights, I believed they might have thought it in their best interest to not inform me.

I don't recall experiencing strong feelings of grief at the time my letter to Kadri was returned. He had ceased to be a presence in my life and so nothing seemed to have changed. I had also blocked out much of my feelings for him during the previous three years. Although I thought he might have died, I also wasn't absolutely sure that was the case. In addition, I was totally engrossed in new motherhood.

———————

I knew of no one in Egypt to contact for information about Kadri. At that time I didn't even know the family's last name—El Lamie. My father's background, his family, and his life in Egypt were all a mystery to me. He never talked about it, and though I was aware my mother knew a lot, she too avoided sharing any information. In the style of her family, her non-verbal messages communicated, "Don't ask." Not only had there been no discussion of Kadri's Egyptian background, there had never been any discussion in our home of Islamic beliefs or practices. Once or twice when I was a child, I came upon my father kneeling and praying on the living room rug, I assume facing Mecca, but no explanation was ever given.

Despite this secretiveness about Kadri's Egyptian background, my parents had a beautiful replica of the famous Nefertiti head in their living room as well as two water pipes from Egypt. When I was a schoolgirl, my mother often took me to visit the Egyptian wing of the Metropolitan Museum of Art, which I continued to do by myself when I grew older. It was as if I was searching for clues about my father by visiting Egyptian antiquities. I was also allowed to look through my mother's album of photos that she had taken in Egypt. The messages I received from my parents were confusing to me. I was able to look, maybe even encouraged to do so, but dissuaded from asking questions. I learned to be quiet, attentive, and listen carefully.

In doing so, I gleaned a few things over the years. My father's mother was from a high-status, financially well-off family in Cairo and she had married beneath her station. Kadri's father was a mayor of a small farming village and the family owned a considerable amount of agricultural land. I knew my father had a number of siblings but not how many. He had at least two brothers, and one of his sisters was blind and was subject to "visions" (I wasn't sure what this meant and whether or not these were hallucinations). Kadri, when young, had been a political activist working to rid Egypt of British colonial rule and influence. His mother's family feared for his safety and pulled strings to get him out of the country a number of times. During one of those "exiles" he had a job working as a secretary for a wealthy man in Saudi Arabia. I had a sense, although I can't point to anything I heard, that he did not get along with some members of his family and that he had strong negative feelings about Egypt.

The evasiveness regarding any Egyptian connection even applied to my own name. On a few occasions, I had asked my mother why I didn't have a middle name, since all my friends had one. She never directly answered the question, or she replied that not everyone had a middle name. When I was sixteen, I needed a birth certificate for working papers for a summer job and applied to obtain one. When it arrived in the mail, I was surprised to see that I had been given a middle name at birth—Khalila. When asked about it, my mother shrugged it off, as if to say it was of no importance. Since it was a totally unfamiliar name to me (yet was mine), I pursued questioning her and she finally relented and said my father had given me the name. I later learned I was named after my paternal grandfather—Khalil. And still later I learned that the meaning of the name Khalila in Arabic is "beloved."

I wondered why all the secretiveness. Was it because my father was a Muslim living in the midst of a Jewish family and a Jewish community? Jews then, as many do today, saw Muslims and Arabs as their enemy. Was he ashamed of being an Egyptian because he had strong negative feelings about the country and saw it as a backward place and not up to par with the West? I really didn't know, but it made me think he (and perhaps my mother) saw his Egyptian Muslim background as shameful and warranting concealment. It made me uncomfortable and made me feel that I too had to conceal this information about him. This led me, from an early age, to see my parents' respective religions and cultures in black and white terms; my mother's was all-good, my father's all-bad. This in turn created identity problems for me and contributed to my sense that there was an unacceptable part of myself that also needed to be hidden.

I was aware that I did not physically resemble my mother or her family. I looked very much like my father and was clearly his biological child; I had his nose (oh, how I longed for my mother's smaller, straight nose), his forehead, hairline, dark eyes, hair, and complexion. People often thought I looked Jewish or perhaps Italian. I never disabused them by telling them I looked like my father who was Egyptian. In elementary school, classmates in the schoolyard often inquired about my last name, as it fit neither the Jewish or Italian surnames with which they were familiar. I avoided enlightening them.

—•••—

In her early thirties, prior to her marriage, my mother had been a world traveler. She spent her summers and a sabbatical year traveling to Western Europe, China, Japan, and the Middle East. As a child, I loved looking at all her photo albums of the exotic places where she had lived or visited. It wasn't until I was an adult that I realized how unique she was to have traveled by herself to all those places. In the early 1930s, without any tour groups, travel agents, assistance, or contacts, she traveled alone to countries where she didn't know the language or the culture. What an adventurous and courageous woman she had been!

I learned from my aunt Janet that my parents had met during one of Anne's trips abroad; my parents never shared any information with me about their meeting or their early relationship. According to my aunt, they met in London when my mother had applied to the consular section of the Egyptian embassy to get a tourist visa. My father was working at the embassy at the time. Shortly after their meeting, he arranged for her to visit and stay with his mother, who was then living in Cairo, and taking a leave of absence from his job, he followed her and traveled with her around the country.

I recently told my friend Lisa how my parents had met, and her response was what strong chemistry there must have been between them. It sounded like a very romantic beginning, but that certainly was not the way it turned out. Although I recall happy times together as a family when I was relatively young, documented by old family photos that I recently unearthed and are now unfortunately terribly faded, the good times ceased at some point and I can't pinpoint when in time that happened. What I do remember is the almost constant tension that existed between my parents and their frequent separations. I don't know what their conflicts and disagreements were about, as they both tried to protect me by dealing with them out of my presence or hearing. But they couldn't protect me from feeling the tension that was almost always palpable.

The level of tension varied, and sometimes it became so intense that Kadri seemed about to explode. I can recall one time when he did, slashing a group of Anne's recently completed oil paintings, totally ruining them. Usually when tension became too intense, Kadri moved out and lived elsewhere for a short time. There was constant back and forth movement in their relationship; they seemed unable to live apart but also seemed unable to live together for very long. The tension between my parents, as well as their separations, was akin to the "elephant in the living room." It was never discussed or acknowledged by them, or by my mother's family, who I am sure had a sense of what was going on. Again, this avoidance was very much in keeping with the family style.

I can only speculate about the sources of my parents' conflicts. I would guess that their cultural and religious differences were a significant factor. Although neither of them was religious in practice, they still strongly identified with the religions and cultures they came from. I have a hunch that my father made many requests, coming out of his traditional Egyptian Muslim male background, that a liberated, independent American woman would have found unacceptable. I think it possible that some of those requests may have involved me and that my mother shielded me from them. I can well imagine, given her style, that she ignored his wishes, never discussed them with him, and they never worked together at resolving their differences.

Kadri's immigrant status may have also been a contributing problem. Although he became a naturalized American citizen, the United States was still a foreign country to him, and the culture was far different than the one in which he had been raised. I don't know if he ever associated with any other Egyptians or Muslims and whether or not he felt isolated in this country. His employment as a hotel accountant and night manager was also a far cry from his former embassy work. He had lost the prestige and standing derived from that position and from the family connections he had in Egypt. Coping with this change in status, combined with Anne ignoring his culturally laden wishes, may have fueled his feelings of being powerless, demeaned, and angry. I can see all of this now with hindsight, but as a child, teenager, and young adult, I was primarily aware of his distance, anger, and outsider status in the family.

During my adolescence, a few incidents caused me to suspect that Kadri kept our existence a secret from the people he interacted with outside the family. I was very familiar with my mother's circle of friends and acquaintances but never met, or even knew of, any friends, acquaintances, or business associates of my father. From the time I was ten years old, my mother started a tradition of taking me to Broadway musicals for my birthday. I remember one year when I was an adolescent suggesting to my parents that my father join us for a matinee performance, to be followed by dinner at an Indian restaurant. I knew my father loved curried food. We no longer went out together as a family and this was my attempt to change that (it proved to be my first and last attempt). I became aware while in the restaurant that Kadri was acutely uncomfortable and seemed concerned that someone he knew and saw there might see us together. I don't know whether or not my mother was aware of this; if she was, she chose to give no indication. Neither she nor I said anything about it to one another afterward.

I also remember times when Kadri was expecting a phone call and instructed me, outside of my mother's presence or hearing, to be sure to avoid indicating that I was his daughter if I answered the phone in his absence. I always followed his requests, not wanting him to get "caught." I wasn't sure what this was about and never mentioned these incidents to Anne. I probably wanted to ensure that I didn't contribute to any escalation in their conflicts. I did wonder whether there was another woman in my father's life and if he was trying to hide our existence from her. I also considered the possibility that he had Muslim friends and acquaintances and didn't want them to know he had a Jewish family.

———•••••———

When I was a teenager, I sometimes thought about whether there were other children from Jewish-Muslim marriages and, if so, what their situations were like and how they coped. I never met a single one. By then, I was aware that such marriages were rare and would probably be met with opprobrium and rejection from both groups.

I had always been affected by my parents' relationship, but I had a more difficult time during my senior high school days. I experienced periods of depression and over-ate as a way to soothe myself, sometimes binge eating, and then, of course, I was miserable about being overweight. The family doctor suggested that my mother put a lock on the refrigerator door; I was never sure whether or not he was serious. My academic performance kept fluctuating from high to low, no doubt reflecting the level of family tension. Anne was always distressed and unhappy with me when my grades were in the toilet as she hoped for high academic performance from me. Adding to my woes, I frequently broke out with large, unsightly patches of eczema.

I sought solace two ways. One was by visiting my grandmother and the other was by reading novels. I usually didn't talk much with Miriam during those visits but felt comforted just by being near her and being in her house. For reasons that I have never completely understood, I could barely read until I was in the third grade. Things suddenly clicked for me then and I ran with it; I started reading constantly and have never stopped. Books became a source of joy and a means to escape distress.

Anne was not oblivious to the fact that the tense atmosphere at home was affecting me, and I'm sure it pained her. She knew I thrived, quickly shedding my depression and becoming outgoing, when away at summer camps. She encouraged me to go to college outside of New York City despite the financial hardship it caused her. It wasn't until decades later, when I experienced a sense of loss each time one of my children left for college and later graduate school that I realized what an emotional sacrifice she had made. I was her only child and had only been sixteen years old when I started college. I am so sorry that I never had the opportunity to thank her.

My father was a distant presence to me much of the time. Not only did he make frequent trips of varying duration to Egypt and lived for short periods away from home in Manhattan when my parents were separated, he also worked nights and slept during the day when he lived at home. Although I knew he loved me, it seemed from afar, and we were never able to move closer to one another emotionally. I think we both very much wanted more of a connection, but it didn't seem possible. I may have looked like my father, but without a doubt I was my mother's child. My bond with her was strong, although not conflict-free during my adolescence. She didn't have to say it; I just knew that getting closer to Kadri would have been an act of disloyalty. I do recall one occasion when I tried to broach the issue with her, but she looked so wounded that I immediately backed off and never raised it again.

Anne, Miriam, and Samuel, and to a lesser degree some of my aunts and uncles, were the primary people in my childhood family. Flawed as they all were, they loved me, cared for me, and were the people I could count on. My loyalties lay with them and I couldn't have it both ways.

I never heard from my father after the letter I had written to him was returned "Address Unknown." My husband and I moved from Chicago to Nashville and our family grew to include three children. My belief that my father had died in the early 1960s continued to be reinforced as the years went by. I did not hear either from or about Kadri for fifteen years…until I received the phone call from Mr. Courchaine.

Olwen's Letters

Olwen's letter didn't arrive until six months after Mr. Courchaine's phone call. It was a typed five-page letter on onionskin paper. The letter was long and complicated and I had difficulty taking it all in at one time. In the letter she apologized for not writing sooner, told me a little about herself and her relationship with my father, and described the circumstances of his death. She also conveyed her animosity and suspicions regarding his brothers and the long battle she was engaged in with them. She ended by beseeching me to help her.

Olwen explained that Kadri's sudden death had been a dreadful shock to her and the events following his death unbelievable, all of which contributed to her taking so long to write. "I have just this past month more or less recovered and started thinking of the future."

She described herself as being a Canadian from Toronto. She had taught English at an American girls' college in Cairo and was planning to return to teaching in order to support herself, since she had not yet received any funds from Kadri's estate. She shared that she and my father had met in 1958 and had been married for fifteen years, having married in 1960.

She stated that she knew little about Kadri's life prior to their marriage. She wrote that the last address of mine she found in his possessions dated back to 1960 and she didn't know if my father had corresponded with me. She did, however, know he loved me and thought of me all the years we were separated. "Just the month he died he was looking at your pictures and your gold medal from Ann Arbor."

According to Olwen, Kadri had neither adjusted to nor enjoyed living in Egypt, and she thought that his family was a big disappointment to him, "never like a real family at all." She wrote that Kadri had three surviving siblings, two brothers and a sister. They were: Ismail, age 69, a doctor who worked in a government laboratory; Ali, age 60, a lawyer, accountant, and farmer; and Alya, who was married and childless and somewhat peripheral to the conflicts Olwen later described. Ismail had two sons and two daughters and Ali had one daughter. The brothers and their children were all financially well off. "During our married life," she wrote, "we were happy together and I tried to make up for his family, so we really lived by ourselves and for each other. We were both alone, so we depended on each other for everything."

Kadri died on January 25, 1975. He was seventy-one years of age at the time, and Olwen wrote that he had always seemed younger than that to her. They had breakfast together that morning; he seemed well and had gone downtown to do some banking. He had a heart attack in the bank and died there. Early in the letter, she wrote that she was told he died immediately without any apparent suffering, and she saw that as a blessing. Further into the letter, she related that the police found his brother's business card in his pocket, and since the brother is "*Doctor* Ismail El Lamie" the police went to Ismail's house and brought him back to the bank. Kadri was kept in a room at the bank until 5:30 and then taken to the village. She then stated, "I will never know if Kadri died naturally, or if Ismail and his son, Dr. Khalil (who was called to the bank as well), helped him to die. Some of the family here believe Ismail killed him, and so do I. According to Egyptian Moslem[1] law, Kadri (the older brother) had to die before Ismail, in order for Ismail's family to inherit from Kadri's estate.

"I was at home waiting for Kadri to come home for lunch (as usual) by 2:00 p.m. Naturally I was worried and upset when he did not come home (he was never late without telling me beforehand, we had no telephone). Finally, at 6:45 p.m., Ismail's wife and son-in-law came and very roughly and rudely told me Kadri had died, had been taken to the village, and was to be buried that night. I was very upset and in shock. I asked why I had not been notified

[1] An earlier spelling of Muslim used at the time Olwen was writing that is no longer in use.

while he was still at the bank from 11:30 a.m. to 5:30 p.m. with Ismail and Khalil. I wanted to go to the village; I begged to go to the village to see him. They told me I could not see him and could not go to the village and many other lies. Kadri was buried the next day at 1:00 p.m., while I was left alone in Cairo and read about it in the newspaper. I have since been to the village to see his grave three times by myself."

She related that she and Kadri had been in Hong Kong from 1962 to 1967, and one of the reasons they returned to Egypt was because Kadri wanted to die in the land where he was born and be buried with his mother and father. Ismail did not put him with his father and mother but off to himself. "They said he was a foreigner (because he lived abroad most of his life and married foreigners and had a foreign daughter) and was not a true Egyptian and could not be put in the same grave. I never knew such stupid, cruel, heartless people. And now they want the land and stocks, which have all been bought with foreign money and some of it mine."

She continued that this was the beginning of the lies and the cold war over Kadri's estate created by his two brothers. "The estate could have been settled within a few weeks of Kadri's death without any difficulties, but the brothers are not normal people. They are greedy, thieves, liars, and crooks. All I wanted was my share, quietly and peacefully, and then to return to Canada as quickly as possible. Now it may take years to settle everything."

Kadri had kept his will (leaving her a third of his estate) and other official documents and personal papers in a safe deposit box in the bank in Cairo. Before she and my father left for Hong Kong in 1962, Kadri gave Ismail the key to the box. It was never returned, and the box was empty of all documents when it was officially opened a few days after Kadri's death. Olwen had copies of some of the documents but not all of them and not the will. She accused Ismail of opening the box and removing all the contents, including the will, immediately after Kadri's death. She wrote, "Kadri trusted his brother Ismail, but not Ali. He thought Ali was a thief. He always said that Ismail would look after me. But now Ismail is the biggest thief and the most dangerous of the two.

"Now the brothers have their hands on everything," she wrote, "and plan to take everything, especially the land. They would and may kill for the land. I have been warned not to go to any of their homes or eat or drink anything they give me as they may poison me."

She believed they wanted to drive her out of Egypt. "About six weeks ago, Ismail came to see my landlord, he tried to bribe him to give him receipts in his name for the rent of the apartment so they could take it. Fortunately, the landlord is honest and refused to have anything to do with him or his bribes and told me about his visit.

"I hate living here," she wrote, "and want to return to Canada as soon as I can. My family wants me to leave everything here and come home but I cannot. I must stay and fight. First, because of what they have done to Kadri and are now doing to me. Second, I gave up everything in Canada when I married your father and I need my share of the estate. I am fifty years old."

Olwen explained that due to the absence of a will, the names of the inheritors had to be submitted to a judge in a court of law before the estate could be settled. Ali, according to Olwen, kept finding ways to delay submitting the names hoping that she would give up and return to Canada. As a final delaying tactic, Ali told the judge that Kadri had a daughter whose whereabouts were unknown. He stated that since Kadri had been a Muslim that automatically meant that his daughter was a Muslim and was therefore qualified to share in the estate. Olwen clarified that according to Egyptian law, only a Muslim could inherit from a Muslim. Olwen had changed her religion on paper from Christian to Muslim upon Kadri's request for this reason. (This helped explain Kadri's desire that Mayer and I marry at the Egyptian consulate. He was probably trying to give me "Muslim credentials" so I could inherit his land.) The judge delayed the case until I could be found, and Olwen believed that Ali expected the case to be on hold indefinitely and that she would eventually give up. But she had now found me and was asking for my help in getting her fair share of Kadri's estate.

If I was willing to help, she needed my birth certificate, copy of a marriage document, statement of religion, if possible, and a special power of attorney either signing over my share of the estate outright to her or giving her the power to sell my share for me. She would then reimburse me. If I agreed to help her, she would provide me with more information as to how to proceed.

In her letter, she included the address of a Canadian government office in Ottawa and requested that I send my return letter to that office. It would in turn be sent via the diplomatic mailbag to the embassy in Cairo. She was sure Ismail was bribing the janitor of her building to look at her mail and she didn't want him to see any mail from me. Olwen believed that five former lawyers she had hired had been bought and bribed by Ali and Ismail. Near the conclusion of the letter she wrote, "I am now searching for an honest lawyer, where I will find one I do not know." She hoped and prayed she would hear from me as soon as possible.

I had many thoughts and reactions to Olwen's letter. It was much more disorganized than I've presented and I had to read it many times to take it all in. Even though I had learned of my father's death from Mr. Courchaine, Olwen's letter made his death more real to me and I no longer could block my father out of my consciousness as I had done for some time. I was flooded with feelings of sorrow and loss. I felt much sadness about how he and I had missed the opportunity to connect during all those years he had actually been alive. He and my children had also missed the opportunity to know one another.

The dates Olwen provided in the letter let me know that Kadri had been in Hong Kong when my letter to him had been returned "Address Unknown." I later learned that he had been the manager of a large, upscale Hong Kong hotel. Olwen had indicated in her letter that the last address of mine she had found in Kadri's possession was dated 1960. I wasn't sure if that was my Ann Arbor address or my Chicago address. Mayer and I had moved to Chicago in the summer of 1960 and I do recall writing to Kadri about the move and sending him my new address. We moved again to a different Chicago apartment in 1961 and to Nashville in 1964. So if he had written to me after 1961 or 1962, he might also have received an "Address Unknown" response. I wondered if he had ever tried to locate me all those years we had been out of contact. It would not have been difficult to find me. He knew the address of my grandparents' house, and mail sent to me there would have been forwarded, since one family member or another occupied the family home into the early 1980s. He also had Mr. Panzer's address, and although he had felt great animosity toward the lawyer, Mr. Panzer would have been able to obtain my later addresses for him from my uncle Morris or another relative.

Olwen had written that she knew that Kadri always loved me and thought about me all the years we were separated and that he would gaze at my photos, which he had been doing the month of his death. All this conveyed a sense of longing, but there is no evidence that he had tried to trace me and write to me. Why? The most plausible explanations I can think of are that he saw me as being too closely linked and loyal to Anne and the Rosenblums, and had felt hurt and humiliated by the estate debacle and feared further rejection. He may also have wanted to keep the door on his life in America, which had ended with such pain and anger, completely shut.

I was also saddened that Kadri had not been able to feel at home in his native country. My earlier childhood impressions had apparently been accurate. It seemed as if he had tried to navigate between two different cultures and never felt he quite belonged or was comfortable in either one.

I noted the dates Olwen provided regarding their relationship. She said that she and my father had met in 1958 and had married in1960. I was curious whether they were already in a relationship when Kadri permanently left my mother and whether they had married before or after Anne's death in 1960.

I thought there was a great deal of paranoia in her letter. It was difficult to tease apart what in her account was accurate, partially accurate, distorted, or downright delusional. Did Ismail and Khalil contribute to my father's death? Would the brothers really have tried to poison her to ensure that she didn't get any of the land? Who were these people who were suggesting this? Could Ismail get access to her mail before she received it, thus necessitating that I send her mail through the Canadian embassy? Had Ali and Ismail been able to bribe five lawyers? So much of this seemed delusional to me.

There were other things in her letter that also didn't quite compute. For instance, she wrote that Kadri had been totally alienated from his family, yet in another part of the letter she mentioned that Ismail visited him every Friday. I thought she probably was not a paranoid personality but that her grief and her experience of being alone, feeling unsupported, and financially insecure were contributing to her distortions and delusions.

Despite what I thought to be her problematic mental state, I decided to offer her my support for a number of reasons. First of all, I strongly believed she was entitled to a portion of Kadri's estate and that she was clearly having difficulty getting it. The Canadian embassy's staff in Cairo thought she was in dire straits financially and were committed to helping her. They also appeared to think that my father's brothers were blocking her from receiving her fair share. Their involvement gave credence to her claim of financial hardship and the brothers' obstructionism.

Based on Olwen's description, she and my father had a happy and satisfying marriage. Given what I thought might be her somewhat tenuous hold on reality, I couldn't be absolutely certain that she was portraying their relationship accurately. But she might be, and if so, I felt gratitude and wanted to help her. It pleased me to think my father might have had a happy marriage after my parents' turbulent and conflict-ridden one. Helping her also made me feel that I was, in a small way, making amends; amends for the part I had played in allowing Anne's estate to be handled so badly with my father and for my part in the cutoff in our relationship that had followed.

I also felt sorry for Olwen. She was a Western woman who seemed to not have a social support network in Cairo and was fighting for herself in a system that may have been stacked against her. I did realize that I was again getting involved in a legal dispute over a parent's estate that bore some similarities to the one fifteen years earlier.

In my return letter, I let her know that I was prepared to help her, that I didn't want any of Kadri's estate, and that she was welcome to my portion. I asked only that she send me a recent photograph of my father and, if possible, one of the two of them together. I also asked her for the date of her marriage to my father; I refrained from asking when in 1958 she and my father met or had become emotionally involved.

I didn't think Olwen was initially seeking my share of Kadri's estate, although she must have been pleased when I offered it. I think she saw my position as a daughter, and one who had been honored as a Muslim due to birth, as being a counterweight to what she perceived as the formidable power and influence of the brothers, and therefore a good ally to have on her side.

In my most recent rereading of the letter, now after so many decades, I picked up on things that hadn't really registered much with me before. Olwen, at the time she wrote the letter, was fifty years old, twenty-one years younger than my father and just twelve years my senior. I had tended to think there was a greater age difference between us and I had imagined her as being of the same generation as my father.

I became more aware of the fact that Kadri, according to Olwen, had left her a third of his estate in his will. I wondered why just a third and who were the other beneficiaries?

And, of course, I've thought what a difference the use of e-mail and Facebook might have made. Contact might have been more easily reestablished despite my father's and my moves from one location to another.

———

September 1975

In the next letter I received from Olwen, she wrote that she had not yet received a letter from me but had learned from the embassy that I was willing to help her and expressed her gratitude. My letter had probably not gotten to her yet because I had been away on summer vacation with my family when hers had arrived. It had also taken me a while to think about her letter and how I wanted to respond. The letter that I then mailed to Ottawa had missed the once a week (Wednesday) diplomatic mailbag from Ottawa to Cairo.

Olwen now conveyed a sense of urgency that I send her a copy of my birth certificate, my marriage "certificate," and proof of my religion, if possible.

Due to the continuing absence of a will, the date for the court hearing that would decide the inheritors of Kadri's estate and what proportion each would receive had now been set for October 12.

She said that she had not heard from Kadri's family since her previous letter to me. She wrote, "Ismail collects the rent every month and they keep it." She didn't explain this, but I assumed this referred to monthly rent paid by tenant farmers on Kadri's land.

November 1975

Three letters from Olwen arrived in quick succession in November. In the first one she indicated she had received my letter and again expressed her gratitude. She apologized for not writing sooner but had been waiting for the October 12 court hearing.

"At the court hearing," she wrote, "I told the judge that you were alive, living in the USA and also, as your father was a Moslem, you are a Moslem, as Ali said in April in court. The case was again postponed, until December 6th. You will receive notice of the case from my lawyer, who has sent notice to the Minister of the Interior here. The inheritors of your father's estate are now Ismail, Ali, Alya, you and me."

Regarding her lawyer she wrote, "I received a shock last week when I went to see my lawyer. She is the biggest, most well-known woman lawyer in Egypt. Known to be honest, believes in women's rights, and is a member and a minister in parliament—so naturally I thought with her reputation, she would never be influenced or bribed by Ismail and Ali. Well, it seems they have gotten to her in some way. I do not know how." The lawyer was no longer willing to work with her, and Olwen was going to have to switch to yet another lawyer.

She continued, "I intend to stay here and win no matter how long it takes, and it may be years. The Canadian Embassy has just finished with two cases here (helping two Canadians like me), one case took eight years and the other fifteen years."

At the end of the letter she said, "I am very tired of Ismail and Ali and I am seriously considering appealing to President Sadat for advice and help. I do not intend to spend eight to fifteen years fighting them. I am sure they cannot get to President Sadat, but I can, through Mrs. Sadat or the Canadian Embassy."

She enclosed a photograph of my father, but not one of the two of them as I had requested. She said the enclosed photo was the last one taken of Kadri for his identity card, but there was no date on it. I thought it probably was not a recent photo, as he didn't look much older than the last time I had seen him seventeen years earlier—perhaps just a little fuller in the jowls. She had some recent transparencies of both of them and she planned to have them printed and promised to send me some.

In the next letter to arrive, Olwen thanked me for my note and for sending a copy of my birth certificate and marriage license. She indicated she greatly appreciated the trouble I had gone to in getting them from New York. She had received them at the embassy the previous day.

She was sending me two copies of the same letter—one by regular airmail and another one by registered airmail. (She wasn't using the embassy's mail service as there was a postal strike in Canada.) The registered one included a request for me to appear in court on December 6 and a copy of her letter to Mrs. Sadat, delivered "by hand" to the residence of President and Mrs. Sadat. She was told she would receive an answer to her letter to Mrs. Sadat within three days. She mentioned in passing that her lawyer, Madame Mofida, had been persuaded by Ismail and Ali to work for them against her, and she wondered what they were now planning.

She wrote, "I did not tell you in my other letters that I have Hodgkin's Disease because I did not want you to think I was looking for sympathy and I would not tell you now, only you will read about it in my letter to Madame Sadat. During the past year and a half I have had four biopsies—one after Kadri's death. When Kadri died I had been out of the hospital for about a month (I had an operation last December and was in the hospital for twenty-four days) and was taking radio-therapy treatments. Now I am on medicine, I guess forever. The doctors say I will get better, but I doubt it. Ismail and Ali probably hope that if they can delay the case long enough, I will die of the disease and be out of the way. This past year has not helped the condition of my health, as you can imagine."

She asked, "Have you made any decision about giving me Power of Attorney? Otherwise would it be possible to come to Cairo for the hearing on the sixth? Since the hearing is only three weeks away, would you cable your decision to the Canadian Embassy?"

She added a handwritten postscript to the typed letter: "I married your father January 22, 1960, and I believed your mother to be dead, until you wrote telling your father of her death. I met your father in 1958."

Copy of the Letter from Olwen to Mrs. Sadat

Cairo, November 17, 1975
Mrs. Jihan El Sadate
Presidential Residence
Guiza Street
Guiza
Cairo

Dear Mrs El Sadate,

During my ten years of residence in Egypt, I have observed many instances, which show you to be a champion of justice in all spheres and of women's rights in particular. At the suggestion of a good friend, Mrs. Omar Islam, I am appealing to you to assist me, as I am a widow and a moslem, to obtain the justice that is being denied me by my late husband's family.

I am a Canadian who was married sixteen years ago to Abdullah Kadri Khalil El Lamie, an Egyptian. Kadri died suddenly of a heart attack last January. Since his death his relatives have done everything within and outside of the law to keep me from obtaining the inheritance that is my legal right. I am entirely dependent on the salary I receive as a teacher in the primary department of a language school. At the age of fifty I have been forced to seek employment, although I am suffering from Hodgkins Disease, the treatment of which necessitates my buying medicines continually.

It seems that the aim of my late husband's relatives is to force me to leave Egypt, which I look upon as my home, so they can keep all of his estate for themselves. My situation has therefore reached a crucial crisis.

I would appreciate it if you could grant me an opportunity to tell you in person of the problems I have summarized in this letter. Although I realize your time is precious, I am confident you can assist me as no one else can.

May God reward you for your kindness.

Sincerely yours,

Mrs. Olwen El Lamie
c/o Canadian Embassy
6 Mohamed Fahmy El Sayed Street
Garden City,
Cairo

I had strong reactions to several things mentioned in the letters to me and to Mrs. Sadat. First, Olwen's disclosure that she had Hodgkin's disease made me very concerned for her welfare. I believed she would get better and more up-to-date medical care in Canada than in Egypt. In addition, the legal battle with Ismail and Ali was clearly taking a physical toll on her. I also thought that her illness was probably another significant stressor contributing to her mental state, and I felt she was jeopardizing her health by staying in Egypt and fighting this battle. I now understood why her family in Canada wanted her to drop everything and return home. I thought if they couldn't convince her, I wouldn't be able to either, and she probably would resent hearing it from me. So in my next letter, I just expressed concern that she take care of herself but refrained from making any suggestion that she drop the case and go home to Canada.

Secondly, I had consistently stated in previous letters that I was willing to give her my share of my father's estate and was working on the power of attorney with my lawyer. I was puzzled and somewhat annoyed that these assurances didn't seem to register with her and she was still asking whether I had made up my mind.

Thirdly, the withdrawal of Madame Mofida as her lawyer was something of a red flag for me. I couldn't help but think that she had lost six straight lawyers not because they were bribed, but because they found her interpretation of reality questionable and may have thought her unstable.

Fourth, I initially found myself feeling very upset when reading Olwen's postscript. It bothered me to think that at the same time my father was acting as the injured party and was angry about not being the recipient of Anne's estate, he had already been married to Olwen for three months—they had married in January and Anne had died in March. He certainly had not received prior knowledge of Anne's illness or its terminal nature. I also felt distressed that Kadri may have given Olwen the impression that Anne was dead as early as 1958, when my mother was still very much alive. I understood that Islamic marriage law (Shariah) allows a man to have up to four wives and that the marriage wouldn't have been illegal in Egypt, but Olwen was a Westerner and a Christian at the time she married Kadri.

Why had he given Olwen this erroneous impression regarding my mother? I'll never know and can only guess about the reasons for his behavior. Perhaps he did it to ensure that Olwen saw no obstacles to entering a relationship and then a marriage with him. At a later time, I came to wonder if Kadri may have dealt with his deep sense of personal injury and anger for what he felt was Anne's mistreatment of him by choosing to regard her as dead. Consistent with his not trying to locate me, it may have been his way of totally shutting the door on the painful aspects of that period of his life.

The third letter from Olwen in November had been quickly handwritten, rather than her usual letter typed on onionskin. "Dear Mrs. Zald (despite the fact that I had asked her to call me Joan, signed my letters Joan, and she signed her letters Olwen, she continued to address me as Mrs. Zald), just a note to tell you what I learned this morning from a paper placed in my court file. Apparently the judge has agreed that if you <u>do not</u> appear at court or a representative for you (a lawyer or me with power of attorney) by December 6th you will forfeit your share of your father's estate and it will go to the brothers. The brothers do not want the case postponed again to give me more time to get you to come or get the power of attorney from you. They are winning with the help of my ex-lawyer.

"I am tired of it all anyway and will not fight it. I am sorry you did not trust me when I first wrote to you, but how could you trust me, a complete stranger?

"When you receive this letter it will be too late for you to help me against Ismail and Ali, but if you want to come to Cairo for December 6th or at any time, please plan to be my guest for as long as you wish to stay."

———•◦•———

In reaction to this letter, I immediately sent a cable to the Canadian embassy in Cairo that the power of attorney was on its way, although probably wouldn't arrive by the sixth. It had been a time-consuming process, starting with my collaboration with a lawyer who had written the document. I had it notarized and the document then received a "flag" from the county clerk, which indicated authorization from the state. Following instructions from the Canadian embassy, I then took it to the Tennessee secretary of state for his signature and an official seal. Once that was done, the document with a cover letter was sent to the Authentication Office of the Department of State for yet another signature and official seal. In my cover letter, I requested that the State Department forward it to the Canadian embassy in DC, and they in turn would send it to Cairo. I had been in contact with Mr. Courchaine (the man whose phone call started it all) about the procedure and the fees involved.

I felt exasperated with Olwen for continuing to misinterpret my intentions and communications regarding the power of attorney. I again wondered how much her present state contributed to her distorting other people's intentions. For instance, in an earlier letter she had said, "Kadri's sister Alya came to see me a few weeks ago. I guess Ismail sent her to check up on me." Perhaps that was the case, but perhaps Alya had visited her out of concern and caring and not to spy as she assumed.

December 1975

The next letter from Olwen was dated December 26. She wrote, "I received your cable saying Power of Attorney was on its way and I thank you and I am very grateful for the cable. It gave me the will to find a way to carry on here. I went to court on December 6th and showed your cable to the judge. He agreed to a postponement, now January 17th, to give me time to receive your Power of Attorney and get it translated into Arabic. He said that should be enough time as it was on its way here."

She expressed concern, however, that the power of attorney had not yet arrived at the embassy and asked me to trace it as time was getting short and the January 17 court date wasn't far off. She hoped her health would hold up until the case was finished. She said she was tired all the time and now went for monthly checkups, or more often when she didn't feel well. They were giving her more frequent blood tests but hadn't changed any of her medications.

January 1976

Her next letter informed me that the power of attorney had arrived but there were two problems with it.

"I received your letter with your Power of Attorney, thank you so much. I am sorry I have to send it back for two reasons. I took it immediately to the American Embassy to have it officially stamped and they couldn't do it. Miss Miller, the consul, told me to ask you to use my moslem name instead of Mrs. Kadri El Lamie— write Mrs. Aisha Beryl El Lamie, wife of Abdullah Kadri Khalil El Lamie." (Aisha Beryl was the name that she had taken when she converted to Islam upon my father's request.)

"Second, your Power of Attorney has to be authorized and stamped officially by the Egyptian Embassy in Washington. Please send it to Mr. M. A. Hendrick, Canadian Embassy, Washington, D.C. (personal and air mail and registered) and he will get the Egyptian Embassy official stamp and then send it here. This is the safest and fastest way of getting it back here." She would then take care of it at her end, taking it to the American embassy, having it translated, and then taking it to the court.

She wrote that the court case was now postponed until January 31. She planned to go to court on that date and ask for a further postponement so she could have time to get the document translated. She had taken my power of attorney document to show to Mrs. Sadat's secretary yesterday. He was happy for her and said to get it looked after immediately and then they could proceed from there.

I was annoyed that the instructions were now different than the ones I had originally been given. But as requested and as quickly as possible, I started the process all over again, revised the document, obtained the necessary signatures and official stamps, and sent it on.

I wondered if Mrs. Sadat's office was really planning to get involved in this court case or were they just stringing Olwen along? Or was it possible that Mrs. Sadat's office had already directed an inquiry to the court? From everything Olwen had written, the judge appeared to be fair and impartial and had been very accommodating regarding her requests for postponements.

July 1976

I did not hear from Olwen until July, six months after I had sent the revised document.

"I should have written to you long ago, but I kept waiting for something definite to write about. Thank you for the Power of Attorney document. You must have had to go to a great deal of trouble and expense to get it done. It is really a very impressive looking document. The American Embassy added another page and their official stamp, then the Ministry of Foreign Affairs and the Ministry of Justice. Then of course it was officially translated and then the translation had to have all the official stamps the same as the original.

"Anyhow, after 15 months and 17 times at court (14 times by myself, no lawyer) the judge finally gave his decision, which I officially received on June 8th. I won the case. The inheritors are you, Ismail, Ali, Alya, and me.

"When I presented the Power of Attorney at court in April, I suppose Ismail and Ali were very upset and angry—so Ali put a paper in at court saying that Kadri had told them in 1958 that he disinherited you, because you had married against his wishes, etc. etc. That is why the judge took two long months to give his decision. The brothers must be very angry now."

My father had never expressed any dissatisfaction to me about my choice of a husband or objected to my marriage. However, it is not inconceivable that he expressed regret to his brothers that he had not been able to arrange for me to marry his nephew.

Even though the power of attorney stated that she was to receive my share of the estate, Olwen still showed the judge my letter of September 20, 1975, in which I stated my intent to give her my share. She seemed to feel that clinched the judge's decision. So Olwen would now end up with 40 percent of the estate. She added that the judge said he hoped and wished the Egyptian brothers would learn a lesson. They were too greedy.

She apologized that she was going to need one more signature from me on an official document after her new lawyer searched titles to find what land was in Kadri's name. She wrote that there was still a great deal to do and her lawyer would have everything ready to go back to court in October (the courts were closed for the summer). It would be some time before she saw the money from the estate and she would have to keep on teaching, which she did not enjoy, until then. Olwen had indicated in an earlier letter that it was difficult to take money out of Egypt but implied there were ways it could be done, which she didn't elaborate on.

As time went on, the paranoia in Olwen's letters seemed to have decreased. I thought this might be an indication that she was now functioning better. She was again starting to think about the future. She hoped she could get to Canada for a vacation next summer; it had been nine years since she had been back. The Middle East was too foreign to her family so they would not come to Cairo to visit her. They did, however, continue to be persistent in wanting her to come home for medical examinations. She shared that she had lost seventeen pounds since Kadri's death and now weighed ninety-eight pounds.

For the first time in our correspondence she expressed curiosity about me. "Mrs. Zald, you have never told me anything about yourself and your family. How many children do you have? I would like to hear about all of you and perhaps you would be kind enough to send a photograph of you all." Olwen still had neglected to send me the photos of herself and Kadri that she had earlier promised. She ended the letter saying, "Please do write, I would love to hear from you and would like us to keep in touch. Thank you for all your kindness and trouble. Olwen."

In my follow-up letter to her, in addition to responding to her request to tell her about myself and my family, I told her that my husband had accepted a faculty position at the University of Michigan and that my family and I would be moving back to Ann Arbor in the summer of 1977. I indicated that I would send her our new address once we had found a place to live. I too wanted to stay in touch and suggested that we might arrange to meet in Toronto next summer, as it wasn't too long a trek from Ann Arbor.

After our move, I sent her our new address but received no response. Initially I wasn't too concerned, as there had been a stretch of six months between her two previous letters. I became increasingly worried when there was still no word from her after almost a year, and I again wrote to her. After still not getting a reply, I wrote to Mr. Wallace Brown, the consul at the Canadian embassy in Cairo, who I knew had helped her in the past. I asked for any information he had about her and also requested Ali's and Ismail's addresses if they were in her file.

March 1979

After a long wait, I eventually received a response from Mr. Brown dated March 20, 1979. The letter was from the Canadian embassy in Brasilia where he was now posted.

Dear Mrs. Zald,

I have just received your letter, which was directed from our Embassy in Cairo.

Unfortunately, I cannot help you with any recent information about Mrs. El Lamie as I left Cairo in June 1976. Incidentally I saw Mrs. El Lamie just prior to my departure.

I am forwarding your letter to our Embassy in Cairo for their attention. Any further enquiries should be addressed to the consular section of the Embassy.

If you are able to establish contact with Mrs. El Lamie, please pass on personal regards from me.

Yours truly,

R.W. Brown
Consular Section

Two months later a letter arrived from the embassy in Cairo.

May 1979

Dear Mrs. Zald,

We have received your letter and Mr. R.W. Brown's letter dated March 20, 1979.

We regret to inform you that on June 16, 1977, Mrs. Olwen Beryl El Lamie (nee Ruddy) died in Cairo at Ras-El-Bar, Egypt, at 5 a.m. Medical diagnosis was liver failure secondary to cancer of the lymphatic glands. Mrs. El Lamie was buried in a Muslim cemetery (her religion) the same day.

A search at this time was made to locate you but the search was unsuccessful. The only known relative in Canada was Mrs. Harry Walker (sister of Mrs. El Lamie) who was notified at the time. It is regrettable that we do not have the addresses of your late father's two brothers but trust the above information, although late, will assist you.

We deeply regret the unpleasant news contained in this letter.

Yours sincerely,

D. Kent
Consular Assistant

The news of her death did not come as a complete surprise by the time the letter arrived. She had died while we were in the process of moving back to Michigan.

Poor woman. It had all been for naught.

At the time, I thought I had lost my last living connection to my father.

71

Miriam and Samuel in their early years in America.
Date unknown.

Anne,1930s

Kadri in Egypt,1930s

Anne and Kadri, 1930s

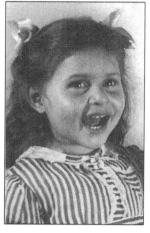

Cookie-Joan   with Samuel

Rosenblum family at Frances' wedding, 1947
Front row: Samuel, Frances and Miriam
Rear row: Morris, Frank, Anne, Benny, Janet and Queenie

Kadri, Joan and Anne
Joan and Mayer's wedding, 1958
Temple B'nai Jeshurun
New York City

Joan and Mayer's wedding
Temple B'nai Jeshurun
New York City

Joan, Alya, Ali, Ann and Ismail in front of
family home in Abusir Village, Egypt,1979.

Joan with female relatives in family home in Abusir.

Joan modelling robe and scarf presented to her
by Mohammed and Abd.

Ann, also wearing robe and scarf, with Alya.

David (wearing gift of galabaya)
with Abd and Mohammed.

Abd, David and Mohammed on porch of
family home, Abusir.

Bahi at Ali's house.

Ann with Fatma at Ismail and Fatma's house in Cairo.

Khalil   Hoda

Nadia and Ashraf

Breaking Out of the Triangles

September 1977–December 1979

I eventually gave up searching for clues about my father when visiting museums with Egyptian antiquities, but I never gave up being fascinated with ancient Egypt. I have continued to be captivated by the remarkable accomplishments of this ancient civilization, and it has remained a lifelong interest. In college, I pursued all the Egyptology courses available to me, and to this day, I never forgo a chance when traveling to visit the Egyptian galleries of major museums.

My study of ancient Egypt's civilization, combined with my mixed cultural and religious family background, sparked my interest in different cultures and religions, which continues to this day. This motivated me to major in anthropology in college, and I spent one year taking graduate courses while I seriously considered pursuing a career in the field. But it was the values of tikkun olam acquired from the Rosenblums and my desire to understand what made individuals and families tick that led me to eventually choose a career in social work. Not surprisingly, once I entered the profession, the developing field of family therapy excited me. The field offered various conceptual frameworks to understand families, particularly dysfunctional families, plus a range of new therapeutic techniques or tools designed to treat, and hopefully heal, dysfunctional families and their symptomatic members.

I was fortunate that the opportunity to receive advanced training in family therapy presented itself as soon as we moved back to Michigan. FISM (the Family Institute of Southeastern Michigan), a new family therapy training program designed for experienced clinical social workers and psychologists, was just getting off the ground and was accepting applicants. I was particularly attracted to this program because FISM had a contractual agreement with the Ackerman Family Institute in New York City to provide the training. I knew at the time that Ackerman was one of the leading training institutes for family and couples therapy in the country.

The training sessions for this two-year program were scheduled one long weekend every month. The training included didactic presentations, consultations on families we were treating (we usually brought in families we were working with for "live interviews"), and family of origin work. The term "family of origin" is used to refer to the family you grow up in rather than your adult family—what I have earlier referred to as my childhood family.

The work on our families of origin helped us have a more personal hands-on awareness of how families function, as well as enabled us to identify our own family issues that might interfere with or inappropriately influence our therapeutic work. This work helped me achieve a greater understanding of the problematic patterns in my own family that had affected me, as well as helped me envision possible paths for change. "Sculpting" served as my gateway to this endeavor.

Sculpting is a technique used to explore both past and present-day family relationships. It is an exercise in which an individual arranges people in his or her family, or people who represent family members, in a tableau that uses spatial relationships and posture to show their emotional relationship to one another. The person setting up the tableau may choose to represent him or herself or be represented by another person. The static positions can also be set in motion to further illustrate patterns of family interaction or dynamics.

This exercise can aid in uncovering dysfunctional patterns since vague impressions or feelings that are on the periphery of awareness can sometimes be made explicit when they are given physical and spatial expression. This increased awareness can, in turn, lead family members to explore different behavioral options. Sculpting is also a useful tool in helping individuals see how they are caught in a family system and how they might want to change their own patterns of behavior.

Early in the first year of training, my group's instructor, Olga Silverstein, selected me to do a family sculpting. I was not prepared, as I had not anticipated being chosen that weekend since there were a number of group members who had indicated a readiness to have the experience. Olga, who already knew something about my family background, directed me to not include myself in the tableau, just my parents. Although I hadn't given much conscious thought to how I would arrange people, once I selected two group members to represent my parents, I very quickly knew how I wanted to position them and how to set them in motion. Once set in motion, it immediately felt as if I had created a valid representation or metaphor for their relationship.

Like a director, I had my "mother" sit center stage with a phone at her ear with a long cord connecting her to her family, who were offstage to her right. The offstage family included both her parents and her siblings. While talking to them, she was also busy oil painting. Her body was turned in their direction away from my "father." He stood in the distance on the left-hand side of the stage looking at her.

Once they were both in position, I set the tableau in motion. My mother stopped talking on the phone but continued to hold it while she slowly turned her body away from her family and looked over her left shoulder at my father. Once he saw her looking at him, he started walking toward her. As he approached, she slowly turned her shoulder away from him and resumed talking on the phone, although she continued to see his movements out of the corner of her eye. He stopped moving toward her, became angry, and began walking away. As soon as he started to retreat, she stopped talking on the phone, turned back in his direction, and looked at him. He then halted his progress away from her and again walked toward her. Once he reached half the distance that separated them, she again turned her back to him and resumed talking to her family. He again stopped and backed away in anger. The interaction kept being repeated over and over and over again.

This was a compelling experience for me both emotionally and intellectually. The exercise enabled me to step back and distance myself from the back and forth interaction of my parents. I had always felt so enmeshed in this pattern and now I could start separating myself from it and begin to see it as their problem, one that no doubt existed well before my birth.

My antennae had always focused on my parents and the shifting nature of their relationship, and this exercise helped me see, perhaps for the first time, the role Anne's family played in my parents' back and forth relationship. Murray Bowen, the influential and prominent family therapy theorist, in his conceptualization of family systems, introduced the concept of family triangles and highlighted the place these triangles could play in family dysfunction. He theorized that anxieties or tensions inevitably occur in a two-person relationship or dyad. These tensions might arise due to conflicts or too great a pull for emotional attachment or fusion. In such a situation, a third person could be brought in to help divert or diffuse the tension, creating a triangle. Over time, if the presence of the third party continues to play a diverting or diffusing role, the triangle can rigidify. Once that happens, individuals in the triangle are no longer able to have autonomous, individual relationships with one another; it is as if an elastic band contains the three parties and controls their movements regarding emotional closeness and distance. The movement of any one member affects the other two, who then have to make adjustments or compensatory moves. In this arrangement, one person often ends up in the distant, outsider position. Such a situation prevents resolution of the initial issue that created the triangle, and self-determination is inevitably compromised.

It became clear to me that my mother, her family, and my father had been in such a triangle. Kadri was in the distant position, but the degree of distance varied depending upon what was going on between Anne and her family. I knew that family members, particularly Miriam and Queenie, often wanted a great deal of Anne's time and attention, pulling her in and thus causing her to distance herself further from Kadri. There were other times when their demands felt too much for her and she sought more space from her family, moving her closer toward Kadri. Eventually, increased closeness between my parents would again cause tension due to their long-standing conflicts and one or another would pull away, usually leaving Kadri in an angry distant position.

I set up a second sculpting later in the year, which was similar to the original one, but this time I placed myself in the tableau. I sat very close to my mother with her arm around my shoulders. Like the first sculpting, I felt this positioning was a valid representation of the emotional relationships. My mother was again on the phone with the long cord connecting her to the Rosenblum family. The flow of motion was the same as in the previous sculpting as she turned back and forth from her family to my father and he approached and retreated in reaction. My mother moved me along with her, turning my shoulders back and forth to correspond with her movements. When I moved away from her toward my father, my mother would gently pull me back. My father lingered longer than he had in the first sculpting and continued to look at me once my mother started turning us away, but as before, he expressed anger and retreated. And similar to the first sculpting, this was repeated over and over again. This exercise was also a very potent experience for me. It highlighted how I had been caught in a triangle with them, causing me to lack autonomy and the ability to act independently.

This led to a third sculpting I did later that same day. In it with me were the same two group members I had consistently chosen to represent my parents. At the start, I was alongside my mother, and my father stood at a distance. I then moved toward him in an attempt to gain his attention. My behavior, however, in attempting to get him to notice me was designed to annoy him. He then came toward me in an angry manner, causing me to run back to my mother. She put her arm protectively around me and shook her finger at him in anger. It became clear in that exercise that the only way I felt it was safe to approach my father was by provoking his anger. Any other type of relationship with him would have been disloyal to Anne. In fact, after doing this sculpting, I had memories from childhood of acting to provoke him, yet never understanding why I was behaving that way.

By the end of the first year of training, I saw that I had been caught in two interrelated triangles, one with my parents and one with my father and the Rosenblum family (which included my deceased mother). Death had not changed the nature of my loyalties. My loyalties in both these triangles had distanced me from my father and played a role in the cutoff from him that followed my mother's death. My earlier correspondence with Olwen had awakened my feelings of sorrow and regret, and my family of origin work enabled me to become even more in touch with those feelings. I also had an increasing awareness that in my clinical practice, I tended to become emotionally involved, beyond appropriate empathy, whenever families experienced a death. I realized that my feelings about the loss of my father were coming out in my reaction to other people's losses.

Although it was no longer possible to undo what had occurred in the past, I wanted, to use Bowen's terminology, to "detriangle" myself. I wanted to be able to get out of the triangles and have independent, autonomous relationships with all family members. I began to think that even though it was too late for me to have a relationship with my father, it might still be possible for me to get to know his family and learn more about them and about him. The seed of an idea of making contact with the El Lamie family and going to Egypt to meet them began to grow. It eventually developed into a clear and resolute goal. A formidable one at that, as it would require that I stretch well beyond my comfort zone.

This goal was further enhanced in September 1978, when Egyptian President Anwar El Sadat and Israeli Prime Minister Menachem Begin signed the Camp David Accords, which eventually led to the peace treaty they later signed in March 1979. I remember being so elated that these two countries were able to achieve peace with one another. I saved the banner headline from the front page of the *New York Times* after the peace treaty was signed and tacked it to the bulletin board in my study, where it hung for many years. I began to think that if peace could occur between these two countries, I surely could make peace with the two parts of myself.

I started the second year of training in the fall of 1978 with two "detriangling" goals in mind, which I believed needed to be done simultaneously. The first one was to locate my father's siblings and establish contact. The second one was to prepare the Rosenblum family for my efforts toward the first goal. I planned to do this by sharing with each one of my mother's siblings my sense of regret that I had barely known my father and that I hoped to connect with his family as a way of learning more about him. I also wanted to reassure the Rosenblum family that this was in no way an act against the family or my mother's memory.

I arranged a trip to New York City to meet with Anne's four surviving siblings: Janet, Queenie, Frank, and Benny. Frances had tragically died just six months after my mother had passed away in 1960. Her death may have been caused by a cerebral hemorrhage although no autopsy was performed due to her husband Leo's adherence to the Orthodox Jewish prohibition against them. She was in her late forties and her two sons were twelve and eight years of age at the time. Samuel died just six weeks later. Many said he had lost the will to live and died of a broken heart. The three back-to-back losses in 1960 took an enormous toll on the family. Miriam survived ten more years and was thought to have been either ninety-two or ninety-four years old at the time of her death in 1970. After a lingering illness, Morris died in 1978.

My individual talks with Benny, Janet, and Frank went surprising well. Although they didn't encourage me, they indicated understanding and acceptance regarding what I hoped to do. Frank even referred to the then popular TV program *Roots*, based on Alex Haley's novel, which he thought was inspiring many people to explore their family backgrounds. Queenie's reaction was of a different nature, and I realized after talking with her the wisdom of having spoken to each family member individually. I am sure that if I had initially met with all four of them at the same time, Queenie would have dominated the conversation and the outcome would have been different. Meeting individually with family members also made me realize that their feelings toward my father differed and that even among those who held animosity, not all of it was virulent. There had been a party line and those who disagreed with it never openly challenged it.

As soon as I told Queenie about my desire to locate Kadri's family, she became enraged and accused me of being "a heartless, selfish, ungrateful daughter." I think she may have even called me disgusting. In an attempt to shame me, she enumerated all the sacrifices my mother had made on my behalf. In contrast, she saw my father as having done absolutely nothing for me. She also made extremely disparaging comments about his family in Egypt, although she had never met them. She was sure my mother was now "turning over in her grave." If nothing else, Queenie was forever loyal to my mother.

I had not sufficiently prepared myself for how I might respond to this kind of tirade and so I reacted with my usual unproductive withdrawal, anger, and defensiveness. But with just a little distance, I began to see Queenie's blatant reaction of contempt and condemnation as liberating. It enabled me to see more clearly how difficult it would have been for me at a younger age to have had a close relationship with my father. Although Queenie was far more excessive than the rest of her family and a zealot on this issue, she was expressing a version of the Rosenblum family position. I would have feared jeopardizing my important relationships with my mother and her family if I had been anything but loyal to them. Seeing this helped me let go of some of my guilt regarding how I had related to my father.

At the first FISM weekend after my return from New York, I shared with the group how my meetings with the Rosenblum family had gone. Everyone agreed (myself included) that I needed to plan another effort with Queenie. She was the outspoken family member and would see any move I made toward my father's family as an act of disloyalty. Betty Carter, my group's second-year instructor, recommended a reversal strategy in which I basically held Queenie responsible for what I planned to do. Betty advised that I tell Queenie that her strong position on the importance of family had influenced me, as she had always placed family first over everything else. I was then instructed to elaborate on how her values shaped my desire to find my father's family so I could learn more about him and about them. It felt like a very awkward intervention for me to attempt with her, but I agreed to try it next time I was in New York. I felt I had nothing to lose.

Although I felt committed to locating my father's siblings, I felt anxiety about what I would do if and when I found them. I feared rejection for a number or reasons. First of all, I had helped Olwen in the legal case against them, a case that had involved family land. Over time I had become sufficiently cognizant of the importance of the land. Secondly, even though Ali had taken the position in court that I was a Muslim because my father was one, they knew my mother was Jewish and probably would assume I was as well. I was aware, although I don't recall how I acquired the information, that my father's family had disapproved of his marriage to my mother because she was Jewish. I was also conscious of the fact that since the creation of the state of Israel, the presidency of Gamal Abdul Nasser and his policies regarding Jews, and the Arab-Israeli wars, many Egyptians viewed Jews as their enemy. I also didn't know how much to accept of Olwen's portrayal of the brothers. She had made them seem like evil personified. In my more irrational moments, I felt a sense of dread and wondered if I would be in any type of danger if I went to Egypt.

Betty Carter coached me on how I might compose a letter to the brothers once I located them. She suggested that I take an apologetic stance for having caused them any legal problems and to act dumb by indicating that I hadn't understood what I was getting into in helping Olwen. She also recommended that I let them know that I feared they would not want anything to do with me. She counseled that if they didn't respond to such a letter, my next move, rather than retreating, was to write again. In the follow-up letter I would say my worst fears had come about and I felt so badly that they didn't want any contact with me.

When I had started on the quest to locate my father's siblings, I had thought that Olwen was still alive and that she, or the Canadian embassy in Cairo, could lead me to my father's family. By May 1979, I had received the letter from Mr. Kent at the Canadian embassy informing me that Olwen had died and that her file had not contained the addresses of Kadri's two brothers. I felt I had reached a dead end and I shared this with the FISM group at our next meeting. And like the deus ex machina of ancient Greek drama, Ginny Sargent, a group member, offered a solution. She had a friend, Irene Gordon, who was originally from Egypt and was in the process of preparing to go back to locate *her* father, whom she barely knew because of her parents' divorce. Due to the parallels in our situations, Ginny thought Irene might be willing to help me. She gave me Irene's phone number and suggested I call as soon as possible, since Irene was leaving for Egypt in two weeks.

I was quite anxious and ambivalent about suddenly being propelled into this situation. On the one hand, this might help me accomplish what I had been thinking and talking about for the past year. On the other hand, I didn't feel quite ready; I thought I might feel better equipped to do this in another year or two. I eventually decided this was too great an opportunity to miss. I might never get such a chance again, and I made the phone call.

I found Irene to be gracious, very intrigued by my story, and quite willing to help. All I could offer her were the names of my father, Olwen, and my father's three siblings, as well as a legal document in Arabic sent to me by Olwen requesting my appearance in court in December 1975. Irene asked that I send her a letter with all of that information along with the court document, which I did the following day. I felt conflicted during the two weeks that Irene was in Egypt; I wanted her to find a family member, but during moments of anxiety, I hoped she would not. I was keenly aware of her return date and stayed close to home that day.

Irene called the night of her return to Detroit. She had located my uncle Ismail! She had first searched the Cairo phone books but couldn't find any of the family listed. She had then turned to one of her relatives; I believe he was a journalist who had resources to locate people, and he came up with a phone number he thought might be Ismail's. She had called the number and initially hemmed and hawed and said she wasn't sure she had the right number. Once she said she was calling on behalf of his niece in the United States, Ismail immediately replied, saying, "Oh yes, I have a niece called Joan in the United States, you have the right person." He asked where she was staying and they agreed to meet in the lobby of the Nile Hilton Hotel the next day.

Irene described Ismail as a delightful older man who was fluent in English. He came with a letter for me that he had immediately written after their phone call. He told her that he was so happy that I had made this gesture and expressed enormous interest in me and invited me to come and visit the family in Egypt. When Irene told me this, I was so moved that I started weeping and cried for a considerable time after the phone call. I was surprised by the intensity of my emotional reaction. I think I cried for a number of reasons; I felt relief from anxiety, I was glad that the family had been found, that I was being welcomed, and that I didn't have to write a letter along the lines Betty Carter had suggested. I also think in weeping, I was mourning my father.

During Irene's meeting with Ismail, he had mentioned to her that my father had been a manager of the Nile Hilton. I think I realized for the first time that my father had been competent in his work life and had had a successful career in hotel management. It was a side of him I had never really known or thought about.

Ismail's letter dated July 2, 1979, which Irene forwarded to me, arrived in the mail a few days later. He had enclosed a Polaroid photo of himself. He looked like a very pleasant man and bore no physical resemblance to my father that I could see. His face and body were longer and thinner, his nose was narrow and not broad like my father's, he had the same high forehead, but in contrast to Kadri, had lost most of his hair. My father had always had black wavy hair and still had a full head of hair in the photo Olwen had sent me.

In his letter, Ismail said he was delighted to have learned from Mrs. Gordon that I wanted to establish contact with my relatives and get to know them. He invited me to come visit them in Egypt. And, if I was interested, he offered to write to me regularly and serve as my guide to the family. I was touched that he signed the letter, "Your uncle, Ismail."

I became very excited about taking Ismail up on his invitation and started thinking about when it might be feasible for me to go to Cairo. At the time, I had a part-time private clinical practice and was also working part-time at the University of Michigan's Counseling Services. The university offices would be closed during the Christmas season, so that seemed the most reasonable time for the trip. I also didn't want to indefinitely delay going to Egypt as I knew that Ismail was in his seventies and I had no idea about the state of his health. I felt excited and carried away by the momentum of all that had happened in such a short period.

I had been keeping Mayer and our two older children, Ann and David, abreast of all the pertinent events that had occurred since the initial phone call from Mr. Courchaine. I didn't think it would be wise for Mayer to accompany me on this trip and he agreed. I saw the trip as an opportunity for the El Lamie family and I to become acquainted and I thought the interactions with them might be different, perhaps more restrained and less intimate, if he were present. I also felt I needed to do this by myself without him to lean on.

My Egyptian background had always intrigued Ann and David, and first Ann (age sixteen at the time) and then David (age thirteen) indicated a strong desire to go with me to Cairo. Their reactions made me more aware of the fact that this was not only my family that I had found but theirs as well. I thought this might be a wonderful, eye-opening adventure for them, and Mayer and

I, after some discussion, agreed that they would accompany me. Harold was not quite five years old, and Mayer planned a trip to Disney World as a treat for him during some of the time we would be gone.

In my first letter to Ismail, I made a commitment and let him know that the three of us would be coming to Cairo in December. Even though it was just the beginning of July, I began to prepare for the trip. I started looking into plane and hotel reservations, acquired tour books, and purchased a good camera. We invited Irene and her husband, Don, for dinner one night in order to become better acquainted with them and for me to further thank her for her help. Irene suggested gifts I might bring to family members, such as perfume and fancy soaps for the women and handheld calculators for the men. At that time, such calculators were highly sought after and difficult to acquire in Egypt. I started accumulating the gifts.

In Ismail's next letter, in keeping with his kind offer to be my guide to the family, he included a list of all of Kadri's siblings. He dated the letter both August 20, 1979 and Ramadan 27, 1399. Irene had said that Ismail's spoken English was fluent, but I found that his written English was not and was often grammatically incorrect. I thought writing to me probably took a lot of effort and was not an easy task for him.

My dear Joan,

Thank you for your letter dated July 20, 1979. I start to write by sending you my regards to Professor Zald, your children Ann, David and Harold and to you. May I write some notes about your father's family. My father Khalil was the mayor of the village. He had 5 sons and 3 daughters. Their names according to their ages are as follows.

1. Said, male, died, and had 3 sons and 4 daughters.
2. Abdallah, male, died (your father) and had 1 daughter.
3. Ismail, male, alive and has 2 sons and 2 daughters
4. Aisha (Ahhaz), female died.
5. Mohamed, male died and had 3 sons and 1 daughter.
6. Alya, female, alive.
7. Ali, male, alive and has 1 son and 1 daughter
8. Ishah, female, died

You can see that the remaining of your father's family are three persons, two males and one female; so you have 2 uncles and one aunt living.

I was surprised to know my father had been one of eight children; I had not known he was from such a large family. I found it interesting that Ismail made no mention of his mother, only his father. He went on in the letter to tell me that the family was Muslim, which I of course knew, and that they were presently observing Ramadan at which time they didn't eat or drink during daylight hours. He drew my attention to the date of Ramadan at the top of the letter and offered to tell me more about the holiday when he saw me in December.

Ismail proposed a schedule for our letter writing, "I suggest to write to you on 20th August and 20th October, and you to write to me 20th September and 20th November." I was amused by his need to organize our correspondence, but I agreed to it and appreciated his commitment to the role of guide and teacher he had taken on. He ended his letter saying, "My brother Ali read your letter and welcomed your trip to Egypt in December. My sister Alya did not read your letter till now, but I hope in the Byram (the three days of feasting after Ramadan) she will read your letter when we meet within the week." He ended the letter by saying he was looking forward to hearing from me and would answer any questions I had for him. He again signed it, "Your uncle, Ismail." I in turn signed my letters to him, "Your niece, Joan."

I informed Ismail of the travel arrangements I had made in my September letter to him. After investigating the cost of plane fares and hotels, I had decided to make reservations with Frommer's tour company for a one-week package trip. The package covered the plane, hotel, transportation between the airport and the hotel, and some touring in Cairo. The cost was considerably less than if I had made my own plane and hotel reservations. At the time I made the arrangements, I had never heard of Mena House Oberio and had no idea how fortunate we were to have reservations there. I soon learned that Mena House was a luxury hotel that was popular with travelers and was located on the outskirts of Cairo, directly across the road from the famous pyramids of Giza.

Ismail's next letter was dated 20th October 1979.

My dear Joan,

Thank you for your letter of September 20th.
I start in answering your questions.

1. *Your father Kadri was buried in the village which my father Khalil was the mayor and where we all grew up.*

2. *It is very good for you to visit your father's grave.*

You will arrive to Hotel Mena House Oberio in the evening of Dec. 19th (Wednesday). I wonder if you would like to visit your father's grave on Thursday Dec. 20th or Friday December 21st and spend - the father's village - the rest of the day and meet my sister Alya and brother Ali.

3. *My brother Ali lives on the road to the village - in his house. Ali is very pleased to see you, your daughter Ann and your son David. He knows little English.*

4. *My sister Alya lives in Helwan and she will be in the village the day you choose to visit. She does not know English.*

He then went on to tell me about his own family. He was married (although he did not give me his wife's name). He had two sons, Khalil and Amir, and two daughters, Bahi and Omyma. All four of his children were physicians and all four were married to physicians. Both Bahi and Amir were presently practicing medicine in England. Each had one son. Khalil was a gynecologist and a midwife (he would be called an obstetrician in the States) practicing in Cairo and had two sons. Omyma was a lecturer at the Faculty of Medicine at Ain-Shams University and had three-year-old twin daughters. He went into great detail about where they all had received their medical education and their respective specialties and positions. He clearly was very proud of all of them. He also mentioned that they all knew English but his wife did not.

As the time neared for the trip, even though Ismail's letters were very welcoming, I was plagued by anxiety dreams. One of the women in the FISM group had shared with us that she felt caught between two feuding siblings, one of whom had told her she had to make a choice and couldn't have it both ways. This phrase, "You can't have it both ways," resonated with me. In my most frequently recurring dream, I was hopping from one ice floe to another and trying to avoid falling into icy, treacherous water. A male voice, as if coming from the heavens, boomed, "You can't have it both ways."

During the daytime, I usually felt excited about the trip, but underlying anxiety sometimes surfaced. On one occasion, with Ann accompanying me, I went to renew my passport at a government office building in downtown Ann Arbor. I had trouble filling out the form because of anxiety and had to take it with me to complete at home. Ann was surprised and amused, as this was not consistent with the super-competent image she had of me at that time. I recall she enjoyed razzing me about it for days.

Right before we left, my good friend Helen, whom I had met in FISM and with whom I shared an office suite, gave me a blank-paged leather book to use as a journal on the trip. I had not previously thought about keeping a journal and greatly appreciated the idea and the book itself. Once in Egypt, I faithfully wrote in it every night no matter how tired I was, recording the events of the day and my thoughts and feelings.

We left for New York City a few days prior to flying to Athens and then on to Cairo. I wanted to have the opportunity to attempt Betty Carter's suggested reversal with Queenie and also to spend some time with the rest of the family. I had something close to a panic attack in the car as Mayer drove us to the Detroit airport. I thought: *What am I doing to myself? What am I getting myself into? This is crazy.* Even though I didn't realize it, I had said this out loud because Mayer later said he remembered hearing me say it.

I did have some time alone with Queenie and conversationally talked with her about how her emphasis on family had influenced me and played a role in my desire to know more about Kadri and his family. She seemed surprised but said nothing and looked a little puzzled. The family had a going away dinner for the three of us the night before we left; Janet, Queenie, Benny, Frank, and his wife, Bea, were all there. Once we were assembled, Queenie started criticizing the trip, saying it was a stupid thing to do. So much for the reversal, I thought. What was interesting was that the rest of the family came to my defense and told her to be quiet.

I don't think this would have happened if I hadn't talked to each one individually on my previous trip to New York. After that, Queenie seemed to keep herself under better control; her questions about the trip had an edge to them but were muted and not blatantly attacking. Perhaps the reversal had done a little good. I felt that the rest of the family genuinely wanted our trip to be a success.

I came close to another panic attack in the taxi driving from Manhattan to Kennedy Airport. I again had thoughts that I was crazy for doing this. Fortunately, my desire to be strong and competent for my children helped me regain control and function adequately.

We had a long layover in Athens, and David insisted that we go to the Acropolis rather than hang around the airport. We had visited the Acropolis eight years earlier when we lived in London for the year and had vacationed in Greece, but David had just been five or six years old at the time and didn't remember much of that trip. Although I felt exhausted from lack of sleep (due to a combination of a sleepless night prior to the flight and the loud exuberance of some of the Greek men on the plane who were returning home), I finally acquiesced to his pleas. I changed an American Express traveler's check into drachmas and we hailed a taxi to take us there. As the taxi navigated narrow, winding streets, I experienced a second wind once I started to get glimpses of the Acropolis high up in the distance, looking majestic sitting on top of its rock base. I was glad we had come.

At the Parthenon, Ann and I were surprised when David, with his dry sense of humor, suddenly had on a T-shirt with a printed picture of the Nashville Parthenon. Nashville has a full-scale replica of the Parthenon built in 1897 for the Tennessee Centennial Exposition. David had known that we would have a long layover at the Athens airport and had hoped I would agree to visit the Acropolis. Just in case I did, he had prepared by wearing the T-shirt under his sweater. I still have a photo of David standing in front of the Parthenon wearing that shirt and looking very pleased with himself.

We barely made it back in time to board the plane to Cairo. The passenger lounge felt as if we were already in the Middle East as most of the waiting passengers were speaking Arabic and many of the women were covered with long coats or dresses and headscarves. A few of the men wore the traditional native garment, the galabaya, an ankle-length, long-sleeved tunic with a collar and open neck. Once we boarded, we found notes at our seats in both English and Arabic assuring us that pork, which Muslims (like Jews) are prohibited from eating, would not be served at our meal.

We were on our way!

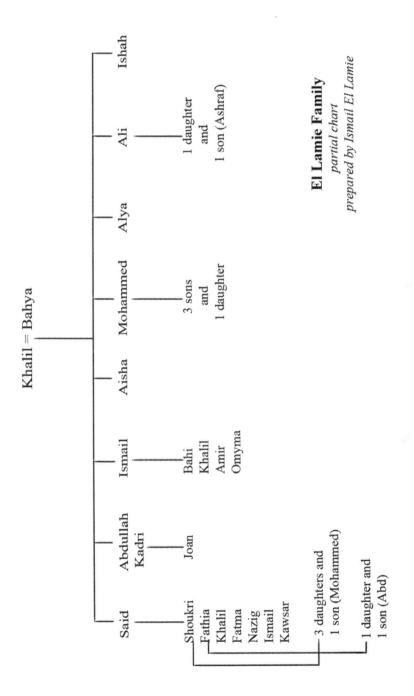

El Lamie Family
partial chart
prepared by Ismail El Lamie

Cairo

Wednesday night

Our plane arrived in Cairo around 10:00 p.m. at night. We had seen the lights of Alexandria from the air and I had hoped we would also see Cairo illuminated below us. I had not realized that would not be possible since we were arriving from the north and the airport was in the northeast corner of the city. We were weary and sleep deprived and I was relieved that a Frommer's representative was there to meet us. He quickly shepherded us through customs and escorted us outside to a small bus that would take us to the hotel. I was thankful for the assistance, as I noticed that most passengers had to wait in long, slow lines and many were having their baggage thoroughly searched. I was struck by how cavernous and empty the airport seemed with only the passengers from a few arriving and departing planes at that hour.

Once we stepped outside, however, I saw that there were masses of people, most of them men, crowded behind metal barriers waiting for arriving passengers. There were lines of station wagons and taxis, some piled high with luggage, and trucks loaded with what looked like bales of cotton. The air was filled with the din of loud voices and honking horns. The presence of soldiers on guard was quite noticeable both inside and outside the airport building. They appeared somewhat bedraggled in comparison to American soldiers, but their weapons, which included bayonets, looked lethal. I had noticed when we boarded our plane in Athens, and again upon our arrival in Cairo, how much darker in complexion most Egyptians were in comparison to my father. It made me aware that he had been light skinned for an Egyptian. I wondered if that was also true for the rest of his family.

Ann and David immediately fell asleep once the bus started moving. We drove through some neighborhoods that were in total darkness, seemingly lacking any electricity, and then through other neighborhoods that were well lit and crowded with people. In those areas, coffee shops were busy with patrons and customers crowded into small, narrow stores that looked like cells. Each store appeared to specialize in just a single type of product, such as meat or produce or canned goods. We passed what I later learned were the Alabaster Mosque and The Citadel, both dramatically lit up against the night sky.

My memory of our arrival at Mena House is foggy as I was so tired. We immediately collapsed into bed as we planned to join an early-morning tour of the pyramids. I didn't think Ismail, who knew of our late arrival, would be calling us too early in the morning.

I realized before I fell asleep that I had forgotten to buy bottled water as we had been told that the tap water was unsafe to drink.

Thursday

We got up at the crack of dawn in order to be on time for the tour. The weather forecasts that I had been following before we left the States had indicated that the weather was chilly and cloudy with some rain. We were very fortunate as the weather had changed for the better and it was now a sunny day with a clear blue sky. We had some time before meeting our tour group and spent it exploring the hotel and the grounds. The hotel far exceeded my expectations. The original section was palatial with arabesque décor, balconies with mashrabiya screens, handcrafted wood furniture, and rich, luxurious, decorative fabrics. The grounds behind the hotel included a large swimming pool and extensive, well-cared for, jasmine-smelling gardens. Visible from most hotel windows and gardens were the three looming Giza pyramids, dwarfing everyone and everything in sight. Once we stepped out the front door with our tour group, it was striking to see that the land directly across the road from our greenery-surrounded hotel was desert. In addition to the three of us, there were just a few other people in our group. Although we were all quite capable of walking across the road, our guide insisted that we go to the camel and horse garage next to the hotel for our transportation to the pyramids.

Ann, who had some experience horseback riding, selected a horse, and David chose a camel. I was led to a horse-drawn carriage but requested a camel instead as I had never ridden one and wanted the experience. The ride felt much like being on a boat with a rolling sea under me. I had seen pictures of the Giza pyramids and the Sphinx most of my life, but the pictures never included busloads of tourists and swarms of vendors hawking postcards, jewelry, and various other souvenirs. Nonetheless, it felt thrilling, almost electrifying, to finally experience the real thing. These were truly amazing, massive structures from ancient Egypt's Old Kingdom dating back to as early as 2700 BCE. The guide gave us his prepared talk. Each pyramid was for a different Fourth Dynasty pharaoh; the Great Pyramid, the oldest and largest, was for Pharaoh Khufu (also known by his Greek name Cheops), the second one was for his son Khafre, and the third and smallest one was for Khafre's son Menkaure. These were burial tombs from which the pharaohs, along with their entourage of people and possessions, were believed to journey to the afterworld.

The group was given the choice of going into either the Khufu or the Khafre pyramid. We chose the latter because some the passageways in Khufu required crawling. Going through Khafre wasn't too easy either; most of our time was spent in hieroglyphic-decorated passageways that were narrow with low roofs, requiring that we bend over much of the way. The air was very stuffy, and I think we all felt relieved when we finally emerged and were able to breathe fresh air. It was midmorning by the time we exited Khafre; the earlier morning chill was gone and the day had begun to heat up. I felt we needed to get back to the hotel to receive Ismail's call. This time we just walked across the road to the hotel.

The phone rang a few minutes after we had settled back in our room. A male voice on the other end said in English, "This is Professor El Lamie and we are waiting in the reception area to greet you." I wasn't sure if it was Ismail or his son Khalil on the phone or who the "we" included. I later decided it was Khalil who had called. I was surprised that Ismail hadn't called first from his home. I said we would be right down and we quickly washed up. I was extremely nervous as we walked through the long hotel corridors to get to the reception area. I immediately recognized Ismail from his photograph. He was sitting with a man and woman whom I thought to be in their late thirties or early forties. They were dressed in Western clothes, the woman had reddish-blonde hair (which I later realized was not her natural color), and their skin color, like my father's, was light for Egyptians. They looked like European tourists who might be staying at the hotel. The man with Ismail slightly resembled my father and I assumed he was Khalil. I wasn't sure who the woman was and at first believed she was Khalil's wife. She turned out to be Bahi, Ismail's oldest child, who I had thought was in England. Fortunately for us, they all spoke English fluently.

They, of course, immediately knew who we were and greeted us warmly. Ismail explained that the phones were not working in Cairo so they had driven out to meet us without being able to call first. He also mentioned that his phone had ceased to work for five months starting the day after Mrs. Gordon had called him. So we might not have met if she had tried to call one day later!

Ismail impressed me as being a very kind and gracious man and he clearly wanted this meeting to go well. He need not have worried, as the conversation from the very start flowed easily and smoothly. Bahi had a teenage son, Hesham, who was around Ann's age, and Khalil had two sons; the eldest, Ismail, was thirteen, so they were very familiar and comfortable with teenagers. They asked Ann and David about their interests and activities, and I felt very proud to have such interesting, socially sensitive, and poised children. David, Khalil, and Ismail had a long conversation about soccer, sports apparently being a vehicle for male bonding throughout the world.

I found Bahi to be lively, warm, and friendly, and I immediately liked her. She explained that she was presently in Cairo for a few months for additional medical training while her husband and son remained at home in England. Both she and her husband had been living and working in England for the past twenty years and she was in the process of becoming a British citizen. She spoke of the difficulty she was having with the naturalization authorities, as they were not familiar with the practice of Egyptian women keeping their family names and kept expecting her to use her husband's surname on official documents.

We talked of the changes she had seen in Egypt since she first left twenty years ago. She was struck by the Islamic revival and how women were now dressing in more conservative style, wearing long dresses and coats and covering their arms and hair. She was surprised to see this occurring even at the university level. She feared the revival might lead to fanaticism and expressed hope that it was all just a passing fad.

There had been a conference between Israelis and Egyptians at the hotel that had ended just before we arrived, and that led to our discussion of the Israeli/Egyptian peace treaty. I realized as we talked that although we all felt positive about the treaty, we viewed its significance differently. Its importance for me was the achievement of peace between a Jewish and Muslim country; that seemed secondary to them. Of prime importance to all three of them was the opportunity to redirect money from the defense budget to much needed domestic projects. They spoke with great concern of the poverty, low literacy rate, and expanding population in the country. At that time, the population of Egypt was approximately forty million with ten million people living in Cairo. It is more than double that today.

Bahi knew that we would be going to the village the next day and seemed bothered that my children were going with me. She was reluctant to verbalize her concerns, and I sensed that Ismail's presence might have prevented her from doing so. I wondered if she didn't want my children to meet family members who lived in a village that she considered backward and poor. Perhaps it was a source of embarrassment to her. I had no intentions of changing our plans, especially since she couldn't give me specific reasons to do so. It was also not my style to prevent my children from seeing poverty or cultures that were different from our own. I was very much my mother's daughter in this respect and thought it important to expand my children's social awareness.

We talked for about two hours before they got up to leave. Ismail and I firmed up our plans for the next day's trip to the village. I thought things had gone well for a get-acquainted meeting. It had been low-key, friendly, comfortable, and interesting.

Later in the afternoon after we had rested, we decided to go on what was advertised as an "Islamic Tour," which took us to the Ibn Toulun and Alabaster (Mohamed Ali) Mosques. Despite my interest in the mosques, it was this first daylight ride through the streets of Cairo that affected me the most. The images that stayed with me were of streets that were incredibly crowded, teeming with people. A great percentage of the women were dressed conservatively and wore long-sleeved dresses or coats and covered their hair with headscarves. Fruit and vegetable stands were piled high with beautiful produce, and the women who gracefully balanced trays of produce on their heads enthralled me. Traffic was very heavy and streets were clogged with cars and buses. Drivers were constantly changing lanes in hopes of getting into one that moved, and horns blared constantly. Passengers were tightly packed in buses and I wondered how people managed to breathe in them.

I had some familiarity with poverty in America from past work experiences, but I had never encountered the type of third world urban poverty that existed in some of the neighborhoods we drove through. People were living in small, flimsy shacks or mud hovels without running water, toilet facilities, or electricity. We drove past the City of the Dead, which was a cemetery as large as a small city, where we could see homeless families camped out among the graves. Poor children begging with outstretched hands, yelling "baksheesh, baksheesh," constantly besieged us. I began to grasp the severity of the domestic problems that Ismail, Khalil, and Bahi had talked about earlier in the day.

In the evening back at the hotel, removed from the cacophony of the city, I was able to reflect on what a momentous day it had been. I had visited the Giza pyramids and Sphinx, as well as seen something of present-day Cairo. I had always hoped to see these pyramids one day, but it had been more of a pipe dream for some distant time in the future. I could barely believe I was here and that the reality had measured up to the dream. Most important of all, we had met my uncle and two cousins. I liked all three and thought the meeting had gone well. It had allayed some of my anxieties, and I now felt a little more relaxed about having embarked upon this venture. I looked forward to the next day.

Friday

My uncle Ali, with Ismail in the passenger seat, picked us up at exactly 10:00 a.m. for our trip to the village. Ali seemed delighted to meet us. I was taken by surprise as he looked uncannily like my father. He did not speak English, but as time went on, I had the impression that he understood some of our conversation. He was a quiet man, but that may have been due in part to the language barrier. Ismail served as our interpreter during the ride and throughout much of the day. In looking at the photos I have of that day, I am struck by how we were dressed for our village trip. Both Ali and Ismail wore business suits with white shirts and ties. I wore my usual professional clothes, a skirt and fancy blouse with hose and shoes with two-inch heels. I imagine that if it were today, we would have dressed in a more casual and comfortable manner.

It was about a twelve-mile drive from Mena House to the village. Ali appeared to be a very relaxed driver, and Ismail mentioned that his brother went home for lunch daily and therefore drove back and forth between his house on the outskirts of the village and Cairo twice a day. The road to Sakkara, which we were on, ran along an irrigation canal. Sakkara is known for the ancient Egyptian Third Dynasty step pyramid. The land to our right was under cultivation, and we passed carts piled high with produce all along the route. The villages we drove by were filled with life; there were people everywhere in addition to donkeys, camels, and buffalo. The villages primarily consisted of small mud huts with straw roofs and appeared to be very poor. Two of the villages had handwoven tapestries on display, and I assumed they were for sale for tourists visiting Sakkara and Memphis farther south. Ali constantly rode his horn as both a warning and a greeting.

We eventually took a right turn off the main road onto one that headed west toward the Sakkara pyramids. A smaller road soon branched off, taking us directly into the village. Just before entering the village, Ali indicated that we were passing his house. I had been looking in the other direction and missed seeing it, but Ismail reassured me that we would be visiting there later in the day.

Ali honked his horn in greeting to the villagers he passed as we drove in. I had learned on our ride that the village is called Abusir. (Abusir is very close to a group of Fourth Dynasty pyramids, and in some books these pyramids are referred to as the Abusir pyramids). I saw only one car other than Ali's during our time in the village. Most of the Abusir houses were made of mud bricks with straw roofs but were considerably larger than the ones we had seen along our route, and some even had two stories. As we drove by, I couldn't help but look into the doorways of houses and saw that people shared their homes with field animals. A few women were sitting outside their houses selling produce, and I marveled at the enormous size of the cauliflower and cabbage; they were at least three times larger than those sold in American supermarkets. Large black flies were plentiful, but the women didn't seem bothered by them and made no attempt to swat them away.

The family's house was large and considerably more substantial than the other houses in the village. It was two stories with a sizeable porch and tall front windows. The exterior of the house was painted yellow, and the shutters and trim around the front door and windows were green. I noticed that the front glass windows all had protective metal bars on them. Since I only saw the front exterior and interior of the house, I don't know if all the windows in the house were covered with protective bars. The house clearly indicated that the family was more prosperous and of higher status than the rest of the village. This was definitely not a family that shared its home with animals. My first cousin Shoukri and his family occupied the house. Shoukri was the eldest son of Said, my father's eldest brother, who was long deceased. An area in the front yard was reserved for Ali's car, and wooden chairs were set up nearby in anticipation of our arrival.

The first person to greet me was my aunt Alya, who immediately embraced me. She kept hugging and kissing me, touching my face and arms as if to assure herself that I was indeed real. I felt overwhelmed by the warmth of her reception. Alya looked like a traditional village woman although she no longer lived in the village and resided with her husband in a Cairo suburb. She had a round face, wore no makeup, was dressed in a long gray coat, covered her hair with a black scarf, and was in great need of dental care, as she was missing two of her front teeth. She was close in age to Ali, who was in his sixties, but she looked much older. Shoukri, whom I thought to be in his late forties or early fifties, was welcoming but kept his distance and didn't try to talk with me or to either of his uncles, although he treated them with respect. I sensed there was some tension between him and Ismail. In addition to Alya and Shoukri, there were two young men, probably in their twenties, waiting outside to greet us—Mohammed, who was Shoukri's son, and Abd (short for Abdullah), Mohammed's cousin. They, along with Shoukri, wore galabayas.

A woman I thought might be Shoukri's wife, although she was not introduced to us, came out on the porch and invited us into the house for tea. There were three other women who served us, two younger ones who were in their late teens or early twenties and an older woman, perhaps in her late forties or fifties. I found it difficult to estimate the ages of village women, for they tended to look older than their chronological years. Again, no introductions were made, and so I wasn't sure if they were family members or servants. The tea was far too sweet for me, but I tried to drink some out of politeness.

Ismail, who seemed to have a plan for the day in mind, soon indicated that it was time for us to visit the cemetery. Shoukri led the way, and Ismail, Ali, Mohammed, Abd, and the three of us all followed him. Alya did not accompany us and stayed back at the house. The cemetery was on the edge of the village bordering the desert. The family's section was large and gated. I thought both the size of the enclosure and the locked gate were probably indicative of the family's prominent position in the village. Shoukri, who appeared to be in charge of the family's enclosure, unlocked the gate for us. The gravestones were all of limestone, and Ismail pointed out both my father's and grandfather's graves. He mentioned that Olwen was buried in Cairo in a plot that belonged to his mother's family. He implied that there was a long story to it but never got around to telling me.

I had made the request to visit my father's gravesite in one of my letters to Ismail. I think I was anticipating it would evoke some emotional reaction, perhaps elicit feelings of grief. But I didn't feel anything in particular while there; it just served to confirm that my father was dead and was buried there and that he had not been shunted to the side as Olwen had written. As we walked away, Ismail expressed concern that Shoukri was not taking adequate care of the family graves. I wasn't sure what he saw as the problem.

We then climbed the hills above the cemetery and were met with an unexpected and amazing sight. Not only did we have a view of the entire village, we had a view of the three sets of pyramids, the Sakkara pyramids, the Fourth Dynasty Abusir pyramids, and the Giza pyramids in the distance. Wow! What a spectacular panorama! From the height of the hills, we also could clearly see the sharp demarcation between the green cultivated land and the desert; a person could easily stand with one foot planted in each.

Upon our return, we all settled in the chairs that had been set out for us in front of the house. It had been windy and somewhat chilly in the hills, but the front of the house, which was protected from the wind, was sunny and warm. Alya sat next to me and indicated she had something she wanted to show me. She brought out a package wrapped in numerous layers of plastic and slowly, carefully, almost tenderly, began to unwind the wrapping. Eventually exposed at the core of the package was a collection of black-and-white photographs. She handed them to me, and to my astonishment I saw that the photographs, with one exception, were of ME! Kadri had apparently sent her pictures documenting different stages of my early life from childhood into late adolescence, and Alya had obviously cherished and carefully preserved them. I was aware that Alya had no children of her own. The one remaining photo was of my parents, taken in Egypt sometime early in their relationship. The photographer had captured the two of them looking very happy together.

I was so moved that this woman, my aunt Alya, whose existence I had not even know about until I learned of her in Olwen's letters, had been following my early life with these treasured photographs. I started weeping, much as I had when Irene Gordon had called me with her message from Ismail. Alya too started crying, and we fell into each other's arms. In Arabic, she seemed to be saying, "At last we meet."

Once we physically parted after we had stopped crying and hugging one another, I felt as if I had undergone a transformation. Something in me had lightened and I began to feel far more relaxed and comfortable than I had felt earlier in the visit. I sensed that the others had been moved by what had transpired and that the emotional atmosphere had also shifted for them.

The mood turned jocular, and Mohammed and Abd brought out a white galabaya for David and insisted that he put it on; it fit him perfectly. They joked with him about teaching him how to sit and eat like an Arab, all of which he accepted with good humor. Then, with much joking and fanfare, they brought out a traditional black dress and scarf for me to put on over my clothes. After I modeled the outfit for them, Ann was encouraged to do the same. Alya then presented both of us with gifts. She gave me a necklace that I believe had been hers, which I immediately put on. Ann received a ring, a scarf, and kohl for her eyes. The clothes that they had us try on, which matched their own, plus the gifts, seemed to be their way of embracing and welcoming us into their family. David and I took turns taking group photos and I promised I would send them all copies.

In response to my request, Ismail, with help from Alya, put together a modified family chart. In looking at it, I saw that I had seventeen first cousins on my father's side, in contrast to the two I had on my mother's side. Once they were finished with the chart, Ali, with Ismail translating, asked me, "Joan, did you know that your mother lived in this house for a year?"

I was shocked. My mother had never said a word about it to me. Nor had my father. Why had she never told me? I assumed that would have been in the mid-1930s. I'm not sure the house would have had electricity then and I wasn't even sure it had indoor plumbing now. The village, as far as I could see from our walk to and from the cemetery as well as the drive when we came in, seemed devoid of a community center, a health clinic, or even a small store. There may have been a small schoolroom somewhere, but I didn't see one. Perhaps the children were bused elsewhere to school. All I had seen were poor domiciles for the villagers and their animals. It must have been much the same when my mother was here. I assume there would have been many family members living in the house, yet my mother never gave me any indication that she could speak or understand a single word of Arabic. It was hard to imagine how my mother, a cosmopolitan New Yorker, had managed to spend her time in this village for an entire year. Why didn't they live in Cairo? What kept them in the village? I was so stunned I couldn't gather my wits sufficiently to ask any questions.

Ali's question seemed to prompt Ismail to share some information with me about my father. He related that Kadri had left Cairo University when he was still a student in order to work for a prince in Saudi Arabia. I thought this fit with what I had overheard as a child about Kadri being sent out of the country to work for a rich man. According to the story, it had been arranged by his mother's family because of their concern for his safety due to his political activism.

Ismail thought my father's Saudi Arabian experience had given him a taste for luxury and that was why he eventually moved to

London. It seemed somewhat ironic to me that a man who had been politically active against the British had chosen to live and work in London. Ismail implied that Kadri was not fond of Egypt and found it backward, which was also consistent with earlier things I had heard. I learned for the first time that my father had officially changed his name to Arthur Kadri while in London.

My uncle described my father as being a very private person who didn't readily communicate his feelings to family members. Ismail did say that he visited him regularly when Kadri lived in Cairo, and it appeared to me that their relationship was one of affection and trust. This made me think that Olwen had exaggerated the level of Kadri's alienation from his family. He seemed to have had a strong bond with Ismail and perhaps with Alya as well.

We were called into the house for lunch. A large table was set in what seemed to me to be an entry foyer. As the guest of honor, I was seated at the head of the table in a gilded, ornately decorated chair (the only one of its kind at the table). I felt as if I had been placed on a throne. The four women in the house served us but did not sit with us. Alya sat kitty-corner next to me rather than at a full place setting. I thought she normally didn't sit at the table with the men but wanted to be with me for this occasion and this was a type of compromise. Sitting at the table in addition to Alya and the three of us were Ismail, Ali, Shoukri, Mohammed, and Abd. Before we ate, the two young women brought around a bowl, a pitcher of water, and soap. One of them held the bowl while the other poured water so that we could each wash and rinse our hands. This ritual was repeated after we finished eating.

The table held an enormous amount of food and reminded me of the Rosenblums' Thanksgiving Day feasts. There was soup, chicken, buffalo meat, cabbage stuffed with rice, a pasta dish, several vegetables, bread, and more. The women had clearly put a great deal of work into the meal's preparation.

I had some initial concern about the drinking water, but the three of us drank the water that was served, as we were very thirsty and also because I thought it would be considered rude to not do so. Fortunately, neither my children nor I experienced any ill effects afterward. Alya kept shoveling food onto my plate, far more than I could possibly manage to eat. She reminded me of my grandmother who would do the same thing, saying in Yiddish, "Eat, child, eat." Alya actually reminded me of Miriam in many ways, which is probably why I took to her so readily. They both seemed to be simple, kind, nurturing women.

During the course of the meal, it became clear to me that the four women who were waiting on us were all family members. I thought the fact that I was not told their names or introduced to them was probably a cultural practice, but I was nonetheless bothered by it and by what I experienced as the subservient role of the women. As the meal drew to a close, I asked Ismail if he would be willing to interpret a message I wanted to convey to the women. He agreed and called them in. I first thanked them for their hospitality and the wonderful meal they had prepared. I then expressed a desire that they join us after the meal. Their faces lit up, they seemed delighted and indicated that we would go into the adjoining parlor. I had anticipated that the men would come in as well, but only Ismail joined us in his role as interpreter. So it was a social get-together just for women. Although I had been honored at a luncheon with men, there would be no socializing between the sexes for the village women.

The walls of the parlor were painted blue, a color traditionally used to ward off evil spirits, and the room was very sparsely furnished. There were a few couches and tables, no carpets, no decorations on the walls, no reading materials or personal items or mementos. There was a small radio that one of the women turned on upon entering, which provided us with soft background music.

The two younger women had changed into fancier clothes and were now wearing dresses of the same floral material, and one of them wore a matching headscarf. The older woman who had seemed in charge was indeed Shoukri's wife, Rashida. I learned that the other older woman was Abd's mother and Shoukri's sister Fathia (so she too was a first cousin of mine!). The young woman with the headscarf was Mohammed's wife and the one without her hair covered, whom I assumed wasn't married, was Shoukri's daughter, Alya. They had brought with them another sugary drink, this time made with oranges. I again found it far too sweet, but again, out of politeness, drank some of it. We chatted pleasantly and worked out how we were related to one another and took lots of group photographs.

The women became teary-eyed when Ismail, trying to stick to his schedule, announced it was time for us to leave and move on to Ali's house. My aunt Alya in particular seemed distressed. I hugged them all good-bye, and Ismail, in English and Arabic, kept saying, "Don't get upset, don't get upset." He was obviously upset that they were.

Mohammed and Abd suggested that David sleep over and that they would take him to visit the step pyramid at sunrise the next day. He thanked them but declined the offer saying we had planned to visit the Egyptian antiquities museum the next morning and he wanted to go with us. They insisted that he keep the galabaya as their gift to him. I was sorry to see the visit end.

Ismail mentioned to me as we were leaving that he liked to visit the village at least once a month. He found it very relaxing and a way to get away from the hectic pace of life in Cairo. I could appreciate that. I think he was also suggesting that it was a way to keep in touch with his roots. Ismail, in contrast to what I knew of my father, still maintained an attachment to the village and his background.

As we drove away, I thought about the social and cultural differences that existed in the family. Ismail, Ali, Bahi, and Khalil, as well as others in Ismail's family, would probably be perceived as belonging to the Egyptian elite. They were well educated, had professional careers, dressed in Western clothes, had many Western tastes, traveled abroad, were often bi-or trilingual (Arabic plus English and/ or French) and were financially affluent. On the other hand, Alya and Shoukri and his family had limited formal education and their lifestyle, customs, and values were deeply rooted in the traditions of rural Egyptian villages. They might not be thought poor in Egypt but certainly would be considered poor by Western standards. There did seem to be some upward mobility, however, as I was later told that Mohammed was a university student. I think he was studying either engineering or law. I wasn't sure about Abd's educational status. It bothered me that Alya's brothers didn't provide for her dental care. Perhaps it would have been considered an insult to her husband.

Ali's house was larger and more imposing than any we had encountered either on the road from Cairo or in the area. It was surrounded by a great expanse of cultivated land, which I assumed he owned, and he seemed to have a large number of people working for him. The workers, with whom we saw him talking, clearly treated him as the boss man. Before we went into his house, he took us into his orchard where he proudly showed us the grapes, tangerines, and mangos he was growing. He immediately started picking tangerines from the trees for us to take back to our hotel.

His wife was waiting for us and, as usual, we weren't introduced. I had caught on to the custom by then and introduced myself to her and learned that her name was Nadia. She was an attractive woman who looked to be in her thirties; Ali would have been in his midsixties by then. I knew Ali had a grown daughter and I assumed that his first wife had died. Nadia was wearing Western clothes and her hair was fashionably styled. She spoke some English, and I think she may have been more proficient in French. Also waiting for us was Ali and Nadia's three-year-old son, Ashraf (yet another first cousin of mine). He was a charming little boy and was clearly adored and pampered by both parents and Ali's workers.

Nadia immediately offered us food and drink, all with high sugar content, that she had prepared especially for us. The consistent offer of sweets was clearly a hospitable custom, and although I had an aversion to highly sweetened food and drink, I kept accepting, as it seemed impolite to not do so.

Nadia proudly took us on a tour of her house. I received the impression that she came from a far less privileged background. She kept asking me as she pointed certain things out, "Isn't it beautiful? Isn't it beautiful?" I kept answering in the affirmative, reassuring her that everything she showed me was lovely. She was particularly proud of their TV and their shiny bathroom with indoor plumbing. I was so relieved (as were Ann and David) to see the bathroom and be able to use it, as there had been no indication in the village house that there was any indoor plumbing or a bathroom available for our use. The thing that most impressed me, however, was the wonderful view outside the large window in their parlor. Looking out beyond the farmed land, I could see the desert and the Abusir and Giza pyramids.

Before we left, Ali asked David if he would like to ride one of his camels. He told one of his workers to fetch one, and the man immediately brought a camel to the front door. We (with the exception of Nadia, who stayed in the house and spoke to us through a window) chatted outside while the workman led the camel, with David on it, back and forth in the front yard. Ismail eventually indicated that it was time to move on, and we said our good-byes to Nadia and Ashraf. We were told we would be seeing them again since Ali was hosting a family dinner for us on Sunday. Ismail and his wife were planning to have us for tea the next day (Saturday) and Ali would be picking us up to take us there. It appeared that Ismail didn't have a car or did not drive.

Later that evening at the hotel, Ali's question about whether I knew that my mother had lived in the village for a year triggered a memory of a conversation I had overhead as a child. It was between my mother and one of her sisters and she was explaining why she had refused to continue living in Egypt. It had puzzled me and had made no sense to me at the time, but it did now. Unfortunately, I had no memory of the explanation she had given.

I tried to piece together a chronology based on my newly acquired knowledge. I knew my parents had married in New York City and calculated that they must have moved to Egypt and lived in the village shortly after their marriage. Ismail had said that my father had been unable to find employment in New York (this was during the Great Depression) and that they returned to Egypt where there was a job available for him. Ismail didn't mention what type of work it was and I hadn't thought to ask. I wondered if it was related to managing the land and if that was why they had lived in the village. It was clear from Ismail's conversation that my father had not returned to the States with my mother after her year of residence in the village. Upon doing the math, I realized with something of a shock that this meant that I had most likely been conceived in the village!

This raised so many questions for me. Did Anne know she was pregnant when she left, and was that one of the reasons she returned to the States? She was in her late thirties at the time, and in those days that would have been considered old for a first-time pregnancy. Did she return so she could get good prenatal care? Did she want to give birth in the States to ensure that her child was a US citizen? Was she also leaving because she could no longer tolerate living in the village? Were my parents already having marital difficulties? Ismail did relate that Kadri eventually went back to New York City upon my mother's request and that she forwarded him the money to pay for his passage. In Ismail's words, "She called him back." The phrase brought up memories of my sculpting exercise when Anne turned around to look at Kadri, beckoning him forward. I know my father was in Egypt throughout much of her pregnancy as well as the first two years of my life—a long separation.

I thought more about Ismail's comment that my father was a private person who didn't readily share his feelings with family members. That resonated with me, as he had always seemed to me to be a man of mystery who rarely told me anything about himself. I had also noted how Olwen, in her first letter to me, had said that she knew little about my father's life prior to their marriage, although they had been married for fifteen years. I wondered if he had been able to share more of himself with my mother before their relationship went sour or if he had been a closed book to everyone who knew him. Despite that, I know he was capable of love and that people such as Olwen and Ismail had strong emotional attachments to him.

Not only was it difficult for me to imagine my mother living in the village for a year, it was also hard to visualize my father growing up there. My perception of my father had started to change when I became aware of his successful career in international hotel management. My image of him continued to shift after visiting the village of his childhood. It made me aware of what a long way he had traveled from his roots. To a somewhat lesser degree, this was also true of Ismail. I knew near to nothing about his older brother, Said, but I received the impression that Said had remained in the village. So my father was the first one in his family to make the big leap from Abusir to Cairo in pursuit of higher education.

I had no knowledge of where he had received his pre-university preparation, but I thought that at whatever age he left the village, it would have entailed an enormous adjustment. I wondered how much he had been influenced and aided by his mother and her family. I was beginning to see my father as an adventurous and ambitious man. He had lived and worked in Cairo, Saudi Arabia, London, New York City, and Hong Kong. In my revised thinking, he was no longer just the one-dimensional man on the fringe of the Rosenblum family caught up in an unending conflict-ridden relationship with my mother.

I was sorry I had not been able to ask Ismail more questions about my father during the time we were sitting and talking before lunch. I was interested in knowing more about their parents and about Kadri's childhood. I was also very curious about how and why their mother (I eventually learned that her name was Bahya), who came from a high-status family in Cairo, ended up marrying a man from the village. Their worlds would have been so very different. Even if I had been quick enough to think of them, it would have been difficult to pursue most of these questions as there had been so much going on at the time. In addition, Ismail had things he had wanted to tell me and it made sense to follow his lead.

It had been a remarkable day. I remember thinking that even if for some unknown reason we had to leave the very next day, it would all have been worth it.

———•••••———

Saturday

We started the day by taking the hotel bus to Tahrir Square, the site of the now famous 2011 revolution, to visit the Egyptian Museum of Antiquities located on the square. We later returned to the hotel to meet Ali at the agreed upon time. We continually heard stories about Egyptians having a very loose or relaxed sense of time and frequently making use of the word *bukra*, meaning tomorrow. Ali, however, always arrived exactly at the promised time. We were silent through much of the ride because of the language barrier, but it was a comfortable silence. I told him how delicious the tangerines had been that he had given us yesterday and again thanked him. He seemed to understand me. He frequently pointed out landmarks along the route. It was a long drive to Ismail's house and it made me realize how much driving Ali was doing on our behalf.

We drove through a section of Cairo that was new to us. It looked like a Coptic Christian neighborhood, as the women had on Western-style clothes and many wore crosses around their necks. Traffic along the route was bumper to bumper much of the way. It wasn't unusual for people to run out in front of the slow-moving traffic, and I thought nerves of steel were needed to drive here. Ali seemed relaxed and not the least bit perturbed by it all. He dropped us off after greeting Ismail and his wife, saying he had some business to attend to and would pick us up later.

Ismail's house had a wall around it that offered both privacy and protection from the busy street. There was a lovely garden in the front as well as a comfortable porch overlooking it. The house was large but had very small rooms. It had a personal, lived-in quality, which felt familiar to me. There was a piano, bookshelves filled with books, including Ismail's medical texts that were all in English, a lovely Chinese chess set, family photos on the walls, and innumerable knickknacks, what my grandmother would have called tchotchkes.

Ismail's wife, Fatma (I made a point to introduce myself and immediately find out her name), was lovely. Much like her daughter Bahi, she was open, warm, and welcoming. She wore Western clothes and her hair was not covered. Her hair color was similar to Bahi's; in photos I saw of them from earlier years, they both had dark hair. Fatma apologized for not speaking English well, but I had absolutely no difficulty understanding her. She said she used to practice her English with Olwen when she used to see her. She felt she was more proficient in French as they had lived in France during some of Ismail's medical training.

Fatma called her husband Dr. Lamie and referred to her son as Dr. Khalil and her daughter as Dr. Bahi. Yesterday I had noticed that Alya had both addressed and referred to her brother as Dr. Lamie. Fatma spoke proudly of having nine doctors in the family and quipped about her home being a doctor factory. She joked, although with a touch of seriousness, that I should send Ann and David to live with her for a year and she would turn them into doctors as well. I think she missed having her children around. Three of her four children had lived in England for varying periods of time and Fatma found the separations difficult. Bahi's twenty years in England were particularly hard for her and she had visited her there quite a number of times. Her youngest son, Amir, had now been in England for five years and hadn't yet decided whether he would stay or return home. Khalil, although now settled with a practice in Cairo, had been in England for training purposes for months at a time.

We were offered sweet pastries with our tea, and both Fatma and Ismail were surprised that we didn't want to add sugar to our drinks. On our ride out to the village the previous day, I had asked Ismail what crop was being cultivated in some of the fields we passed. He called them horse beans or fava beans and explained they were used in a popular dish named *foul*. He had apparently mentioned my interest to Fatma, who had prepared a bowl of *foul* especially for me. They explained that it was high in protein and often eaten for breakfast or at sundown during Ramadan. I found it delicious, especially once olive oil and lemon were added.

Fatma suffered from rheumatism and was in considerable pain most of the time. As a result, she seldom ventured out of the house. She had, however, made a special trip to a store where Mrs. Sadat shopped in order to buy me a gift of a silk galabaya. She had also bought a headscarf for Ann. Ismail, not wanting David to be neglected, gave him coins commemorating events in Egyptian history, such as the opening of the Suez Canal and the recent signing of the peace treaty. I was deeply touched by their generosity.

It was interesting that when I gave Fatma some wrapped gifts, she didn't open them and quickly put them in a drawer, barely acknowledging receiving them. I had already experienced the same reaction from other family members when I gave them gifts. I wasn't sure if this was just a family custom or a broader cultural one. I would have to ask Irene once we got back home.

While Ismail was teaching Ann and David Arabic numbers, Fatma showed me a photo album of her daughter Omyma's wedding seven years ago. Bahi, when we first met at Mena House, had relayed Omyma's regrets that she was unable to meet us while we were in Cairo due to childcare issues. Fatma looked much younger, dark haired, pain free, and very beautiful in those photographs.

Khalil dropped by on his way home from work to say hello and let me know that he would be picking us up to go to Ali's house tomorrow. Fatma said she would be going as well since it would be another opportunity to be with us. This would be a rare outing for her. She emphasized that we were now part of the family.

We heard the call for the last prayer of the day from the muezzin at a nearby mosque. Ismail did not respond to it, which confirmed my earlier impression that although he was a practicing Muslim, he was not one who prayed five times a day.

Ali came to get us and accepted some sweet pastries from Fatma to take home. He stopped to buy some food from a street vendor on the drive back to the hotel and handed David a large bunch of small bananas that he had just purchased. On the ride to Ismail's house, David had commented on the size of the bananas and expressed curiosity about their taste. Ali had obviously heard and understood the conversation. Although I was deeply appreciative of the hospitality with which we were being received, I sometimes felt uncomfortable being on the receiving end of so much generosity. This was especially the case since everyone quickly put away the gifts that I gave them without opening or looking at them. I thought at the very least that we should be careful in the future about expressing interest in things that might lead to even more gifts.

Sunday

Khalil had been held up in surgery and was considerably late picking us up. Since the phones were still not working there was no way he could reach us. We assumed he would eventually come and he did. His wife, Hoda, had already driven everyone else out to Ali's house. I had realized by then that Khalil was the nephew my father had wanted me to marry. Since Kadri's plan had always seemed preposterous to me, I had never given it much thought. Now I wondered if my father had really thought through the implications for my life with his scheme, particularly since he had such negative feelings about living in Egypt. I didn't know how much Ismail had been party to this fantasy or if Khalil had ever been aware of it. It felt too awkward to me to inquire about it with either of them.

Khalil seemed to prefer discussing professional and social welfare issues with me rather than personal or family matters. He was curious about my professional work and had lots of questions about family therapy, since much of what I did was unavailable in Egypt at the time. He was well informed about Egyptian domestic issues and problems and we talked at length about them, continuing the discussion we had at our first meeting at Mena House.

Waiting for us at Ali's house were Fatma, Bahi (who I was delighted to see again), Khalil's wife, Hoda (a beautiful, very fashionably dressed woman who expertly accented her eyes with kohl), and their two sons, Ismail and Kareem. We made up a party of ten. My uncle Ismail wasn't present and no explanation was given for his absence. I thought he might be tired and needed a day off from being our guide and interpreter. Alya was also not present. Nadia didn't join the group but kept popping in and out checking that we all had enough food and drink. There was a serving woman in the background assisting her. Ali had discarded his usual business suit and tie and looked very comfortable in the galabaya he was wearing.

The variety and amount of food at the dinner table was overwhelming, a veritable feast. The meal started with a delicious thick chicken soup, followed by chicken, beef, meat patties, a rice dish, a macaroni dish, a vegetable similar to cucumber stuffed with rice, a spinach dish, peas and carrots, salad and bread. This was followed with oranges and bananas and still later baklava, and another sweet pastry was served with coffee, tea, and soft drinks. I was again impressed with the amount of effort that had gone into the preparation of the meal.

This was my first meeting with Hoda, and we shared information about our families and our work lives. She spoke of her career in public health and its challenges and about her two children. Her sons attended a private school and the eldest, Ismail, was already fluent in English and French. He had been to Europe many times and they hoped to take him on a trip to the States sometime in the future. I received the impression that she assumed that he would follow in the footsteps of his parents, aunts, uncle, and grandfather and have a career in medicine.

I also had the opportunity to have a long conversation with Bahi, and she was very open to talking with me about my father. Ismail and Bahi were the two people who seemed most willing to discuss him with me. I thought that they, and perhaps his sister Alya, were the family members who had been closest to him. Bahi mentioned that after living in the United States for so many years, Kadri, much to everyone's amusement, spoke Arabic with an American accent. She told me that she was indebted to him for enabling her to marry her husband, as Ismail had initially been unwilling to give consent. She conveyed the impression that it would not have been possible for her to marry without his permission. It wasn't clear to me if Egyptian family law required that women have their father's consent to marry, or if this was a religious or cultural expectation, or if she just personally felt she couldn't marry without Ismail's blessing. Kadri had intervened on her behalf and convinced Ismail that he should allow Bahi to marry the man she loved. Ismail had eventually acquiesced, especially since Kadri was his older brother.

The family clearly had not liked Olwen, but no one seemed willing to discuss the reasons. Bahi told me that Olwen had chased after my father and claimed that he had promised to marry her. Bahi explained that in Egypt once a man makes such a promise, it is seen as a binding commitment. Kadri initially didn't want to marry Olwen, although he didn't deny his promise to her. He simply discounted it, saying that in the West such a promise wasn't worth much. Bahi suggested to him that marriage would keep him from being lonely and he did marry Olwen sometime after that discussion.

Bahi spoke very fondly of my father and told me that when they were both living in Cairo she visited him on a weekly basis and looked forward to those visits. It sounded to me as if her warm feelings toward him had been reciprocated. I can easily see her with her lively, open manner, joking with him and amusing him. I received the impression that she had been more than just his niece but had served as surrogate daughter as well. She had stepped into the role I had not been able to fill.

The conversation with Bahi had an enormous impact on me, and that night in bed, I allowed myself to feel the emotions I had kept in check during our talk. I found myself missing my father and felt a profound sadness that I had never been able to have the warm relationship he and Bahi had shared. She had made him real to me and I cried for him in a way I had previously not been able to do.

Monday

Khalil and Hoda were hosting a farewell dinner for us in the evening. In the morning, after taking the hotel bus to the Nile Hilton, we took a long walk to the Coptic Museum. Heading south, we passed through Garden City, which was a lovely neighborhood where many of the foreign embassies and the homes of wealthy foreigners were located, and made our way to the banks of the Nile. Stretched along a wide swath of the river's banks were the mud hovels of the very poor. I was struck with the extremes of wealth and poverty in such close proximity to one another. We were apparently a rare sight as we walked along the Corniche; people kept staring at us and schoolchildren flocked to us practicing their limited English. At times I felt like a pied piper as one group of children after another approached us and followed us for a number of blocks. Each in turn practiced their English and asked us the same two questions, "Where do you come from? What is your name?"

After walking by the ruins of a large ancient Roman aqueduct, we arrived at the neighborhood called Old Cairo that was near the museum. It was clearly a very poor neighborhood, jam-packed with people, and many of them gawked at us. I imagine the foreigners they saw visiting the museum usually arrived by tour bus or taxi. After our visit to the museum, a tourist policeman stationed outside the museum insisted that we take a taxi and get out of the neighborhood. He apparently didn't think it safe for us to walk around. We had not felt threatened while we had been walking, but he was so adamant that we got into the taxi he summoned for us.

Khalil was again held up at work and was late in picking us up. We were prepared this time and brought along material to read while we waited for him in the lobby. Khalil and Hoda's home was in Heliopolis, an upscale suburb of Cairo. Quite a large number of streets in their neighborhood were without lights that night; fortunately their street had electricity. Khalil mentioned that the phones were still not working and that it was not unusual, especially at night, for relatives of his patients to come to his home to let him know that he was needed at the hospital. I thought the residents of Cairo I had encountered thus far displayed great fortitude and adaptability to the innumerable breakdowns in their city's infrastructure.

Waiting for us in addition to Hoda and her two sons were Ismail, Ali, and Bahi. Bahi's brother-in-law, who was a judge in Alexandria, was also there and was introduced to us and stayed for a short time. Khalil and Hoda owned the multi-apartment building in which they lived. The apartment we were in was used exclusively for entertaining and was totally separate from the family's living quarters. The rooms were elegantly furnished with oriental rugs, antique French furniture, and chandeliers. At some point during the preceding day, I had apparently mentioned that I had never tried Turkish coffee and would like to try it someday. Soon after we arrived, Hoda had a servant woman bring me a beautifully decorated porcelain demitasse with Turkish coffee. It felt almost magical—I just had to express a wish, one that in this case I hadn't even remembered, and it would be answered.

Hoda asked how we had spent the day, and I told her about our walk and visit to the Coptic Museum. She seemed shocked that we had taken such a walk, particularly through the Old Cairo neighborhood, and seemed to imply that is was not a safe thing to have done. I wasn't sure if I had innocently put us in a dangerous situation and was just lucky nothing harmful had happened or if she and the tourist policeman were overreacting.

The dinner was very pleasant and relaxing, and my uncles began to talk about a return visit, suggesting that Mayer and Harold come with us next time. Ismail also promised David that on our next trip they would have time for a chess game. David had seen Ismail's chess set when we were at his house and had indicated that he played chess. Bahi wrote down everyone's address for me, and since Ismail was the only one who had ours, I gave our address to everyone else. At the end of the evening, Hoda gave me a gift of an alabaster lamp, which Ann now has in her home. Ismail in parting said to me, "Joan, you are now an Egyptian." When Ali dropped us off at our hotel, he had tears in his eyes when we parted.

Tuesday

This was Christmas Day and the hotel and the street leading to the pyramids were decorated for the holiday. It seemed strange to see this in a Muslim country, but I assumed it was done for the tourists. I had originally thought Coptic churches celebrated Christmas on December 25 and had indicated to Khalil my interest in attending a Coptic Christmas service. I hadn't known until he told me that Christmas in the Coptic calendar was celebrated in January. We signed up for a half-day Sakkara pyramids and Memphis tour instead.

On our way to the Sakkara pyramids, the three of us made sure to watch out for Ali's house and the cutoff to the village. The day felt anti-climactic, as we had already said our good-byes to the family. The weather had also begun to turn and was becoming chilly and gray, and it started raining in the afternoon.

In the evening, as we made our preparations to leave, I thought about the amazing series of contrasts, often juxtaposed, that we had seen every day in Egypt. We had had a taste of it on the night of our arrival, when we drove through darkened streets with no electricity and barely a sign of life, into neighboring streets that were brightly lit and crowded with people. Included among those dramatic pairings, which we daily observed, were the ancient Giza pyramids, thousands of years old, just across the road from, and towering over, our modern-day luxury hotel; the villages that we passed on the road, which appeared, at least superficially, no different than they might have looked during pharaonic times and were a short drive to modern-day Cairo; and the desert, side by side with the verdant, cultivated land and always sharply demarcated from it. Other contrasts that made a strong impression on me were the extremes of poverty and wealth, which sometimes existed in close proximity to one another, and the substantial differences in lifestyle, sometimes in the same family, between Western-influenced or educated professional elites and the traditional villagers, as exemplified by the El Lamie family.

Wednesday

I set my alarm for 3:30 a.m. so we could get some breakfast before we left for the airport at 5:15 a.m. The streets were very quiet as we drove through the city although there were people about and some of the stores had already opened. The Alabaster Mosque was still lit and looked beautiful. Our flight to Athens left on time and we easily made the connection to our New York flight.

Once we got settled on the plane, I felt an enormous sense of accomplishment. The imagery I had was of swimming for a very long time against a powerful tide and finally arriving safely on shore. Not only had I connected with my father's family—my family—they had been welcoming, extraordinarily hospitable, generous, and kind. I can't imagine that they would have received us in that manner if they hadn't cared about my father. Perhaps they felt they were regaining a piece of him through us. I came away feeling a great fondness for Ismail, Fatma, and Bahi, as well as for Alya, who held a special place in my affections.

In the course of the return flight, along with my elation, I felt sorrow about the lost years; the years when my father was alive and I had assumed him dead. Those were years in which we could have reconciled, mended fences, and had a different and better relationship. My children would have had a grandfather and he would have been able to enjoy his wonderful grandchildren. I also felt sadness for both of my parents. Their early relationship had held such promise but had ended in such pain. They had both been adventurous and accomplished people as well as individuals who questioned and transcended the constraints of their respective cultures. Unfortunately, neither one of them seemed to have had the psychological wherewithal to deal constructively with their differences and conflicts.

What to make of the discrepancy between my experience with Ismail and Ali and Olwen's portrayal of them? Although she had sometimes seemed delusional about their powers and their malevolence, there was clear evidence that they had not been fair or kind to her in the way they handled Kadri's death and his estate. I had learned earlier in my life, as my grandfather Samuel's relationship with my uncle Morris illustrated, that basically good people can show negative, cruel facets of themselves, especially in stressful situations and during difficult periods of their lives. This may have been the case with Ismail and Ali. They apparently disliked Olwen, were probably very distressed about Kadri's death, and were fearful she would get some of the family's precious land. This may explain, but of course doesn't excuse, their behavior. In contrast to the way they had treated her, I felt my uncles had shown me the best of themselves.

I recognized that members of both my families, the Rosenblums and the El Lamies, shared similar qualities. They were loving, nurturing, caring, and generous, but some family members could also be thoughtless, selfish, unkind, and sometimes downright cruel. The two families were a mixed bag of good and bad—much like the rest of humanity.

I was surprised to find Janet, Queenie, Frank, and his wife, Bea, waiting for us at Kennedy Airport when we arrived. Those were the days when friends and family could meet passengers at arrival gates. They had driven out to welcome us and to find out how the trip had gone. Frank, Bea, and Janet seemed delighted that things had gone well and that it had been a successful trip. Queenie kept asking questions that seemed designed to show the El Lamie family in a negative light, but they tended to fall flat. The old party line that it was disloyal of me to have anything to do with my father or his family, which she had championed so vigorously, no longer had the old power. Her siblings would no longer go along with it.

—•••••—

Family therapy theorists see families as striving to maintain a homeostatic balance, as family members follow certain rules regarding appropriate or accepted relationships and behaviors within the family. These rules are most often unwritten, implicit, and covert (not getting emotionally close to my father was one such rule). When a family member makes a move to change his or her behavior and challenges the balance, as I had tried to do, other family members attempt to get the "disrupter" back in place ("you are a heartless, selfish, ungrateful daughter…your mother will be turning over in her grave."). According to the theory, once an individual withstands the pressure and makes the desired change, the family adapts and accepts the change, and a new balance is achieved.

I was initially very skeptical about how accepting the Rosenblums would be, yet over time they did adapt. Benny, who was always searching through small, independent bookstores, regularly started sending me old copies of *National Geographic* that had articles about Egypt, saying he thought I might find them interesting. Dora, Morris's widow, told me of a trip she and Morris had once taken to Egypt and how helpful my father had been in assisting them with arrangements. Janet shared with me that in the past, when she was leaving Friday night family dinners for home, she often rode the subway with my father who was then on his way to work in Manhattan. She indicated that she enjoyed his company and their conversations. Too bad they had all been in the closet earlier, but they were at least now letting me know they were accepting of the change I had made. Queenie would never be accepting, but her voice was more muted and no longer carried the sway it once had.

As soon as I was able after our return home, I sent letters to Ismail and Fatma, Ali and Nadia, Khalil and Hoda, Shoukri and Rashida, and Alya and Bahi. I thanked them all for their wonderful hospitality and let them know how meaningful meeting them had been for me. I also enclosed copies of the photographs David and I had taken.

Two of the return letters I received were particularly touching.

In a letter that no doubt required great effort due to her limited English, Fatma wrote:

My dear daughter Joan,

Thank you for your letter and photos you sent.
I am happy that I meet you and hope that I shall meet you in the future when you and your husband will come to Egypt.
I consider myself that I am mother of three daughters, Joan, Bahi, Omyma. Joan is in America, Bahi is in England, and Omyma in Egypt. I am international mother.
I tried to write this letter by myself to express myself and my feeling.
My regards to Ann, David, Harold, your husband and you.

Your mother
Fatma

A letter from Alya translated and transcribed by Ismail:

By name of God

Dear Niece Joan,

On behalf of my sister Alya, I am translating her words because she does not know American language. She thank you because you sent her some pictures.

She not pleased with Ali and Ismail because they took you and Ann and David after lunch and she did not stay with you except short time. She is intended not to repeat this again in your next visit whether in the village or on her house in Helwan—a suburb south of Cairo—and you will stay with her as she wish.

She wants to repeat her thanks and her intension that you will both stay together as she wishes.

Kindest regards to you, Ann and David.

Your Aunt,
Alya

In addition, Ali sent me a note, written in a feminine hand, perhaps by Nadia, telling me he was looking forward to my next visit. A letter from Bahi informed me that she was back in England and was now employed at the same hospital where her husband worked. She promised to keep in touch. Ismail, in his letter, expressed the hope that we would resume our regular letter-writing schedule.

———

Upon my return from Egypt, friends and colleagues asked me what I thought I had accomplished in taking the trip. A number of things immediately came to mind. The El Lamie family had embraced me along with my children, and I now regarded them not only as my father's family but mine as well. I had learned a good deal about my father, although not as much as I would have liked. I hoped I might learn more in future visits. I now saw my father in a more positive light, felt more compassion for him, and had been able to more fully mourn him. At a later time, I realized that my emotional reactions had become more appropriate when client families experienced a death. I continued to be empathic but no longer grieved as if their losses were my own.

Something else, which I had not initially realized, changed for me. Although I consider myself a Jew, more precisely, a secular humanistic Jew, I found that I had become far more comfortable and at peace with my Egyptian Muslim background. I no longer felt that it was an unacceptable part of me that I needed to hide.

I now saw both Jewish and Muslim religions and cultures as being filled with riches. I could, and did, have it both ways.

Over the years, Ismail and I maintained our regularly scheduled correspondence, primarily keeping one another updated on our respective families. He now signed his letters "Love, Ismail." I signed mine in similar fashion. He and Fatma were delighted when Ann decided to spend her junior year of college (1983–1984) at the American University in Cairo (AUC). Mayer, David, Harold, and I flew to Cairo during the 1983 Christmas holidays in order to visit Ann and my Egyptian family. This afforded Mayer and Harold the opportunity to finally meet the family and gave David and me a chance to renew ties.

Illustrative of how my children seemed to easily embrace both their backgrounds, David, in 1987, spent his senior year of college studying at Hebrew University in Jerusalem. During a school break he traveled to Cairo to visit with family.

In 1997, David and his wife, Mary, had a daughter and named her Khalila.

If asked today to create a family sculpting as a follow-up to the ones I had done in family therapy training years ago, how would I do it? I think in contrast to the previous ones, which were representations or metaphors of actual family dynamics, today I would choose to illustrate my internal state; the one I eventually arrived at as a result of this journey.

Present in this enactment would be my parents, my granddaughter Khalila, and me. And as in dream states, Khalila would be a changing or shifting composite of many different people. She would represent not only herself but also my three children and a younger version of myself. I visualize introducing her to my father, who would be overcome with joy upon meeting her (us) and upon learning her name. A name that had been withheld and deliberately concealed and now represented an open acceptance and embracing of mine, and my children's, Egyptian connection. My mother would be on the periphery observing us and, upon seeing me beckon to her, would drop the phone she held and come the full distance toward us, with open arms and a welcoming smile on her face.

Acknowledgments

I especially want to thank my daughter, Ann, who graciously took time out of her busy schedule to read evolving drafts of the book in order to provide me with her invaluable editorial assistance. My gratitude also goes out to family and friends who read the manuscript and were generous with their support, encouragement, and advice. They include my son, David, my cousin Joseph Chuman, and my dear friends Penny Tropman, Lisa Tulin-Silver, Galia Williams, and Arlene Wittels. My greatest debt is to my late husband, Mayer, who for years, more accurately decades, gently prodded me to tell this story. He was my biggest cheerleader once I finally got going on it and was always ready to read and discuss the latest draft, frequently reminding me of things I had forgotten to include. Although he did not live to see the book published, I am glad that he was able to read a near to final manuscript.

25629862R00096

Made in the USA
Charleston, SC
09 January 2014